HANDBOOK FOR
BEGINNING TEACHERS

ABOUT THE AUTHOR

Over a period of many years, I have worked with approximately 3,000 teenagers—and am a happy survivor!

I was formerly Professor at Bakersfield College in California and also taught at Palm Springs High, Pasadena High, and other California high schools. I have majors in Social Science and English, as well as a Masters degree in Education. In each situation where I taught (over a period of thirty years) I was offered my contract to return to that school.

I held a valid California General Secondary Life Teaching Credential. A life credential in California is earned after five years of "successful secondary teaching," so I was "in for life!"

My Master of Science degree is from the University of Southern California in Los Angeles, and I have a Bachelor of Arts degree from Nebraska Wesleyan University in Lincoln, Nebraska.

Marian Axford Shea

HANDBOOK FOR BEGINNING TEACHERS

By

MARIAN AXFORD SHEA

Professor Emeritus
Bakersfield College
Bakersfield, California

C H A R L E S   C   T H O M A S   •   P U B L I S H E R
Springfield • Illinois • U.S.A.

Published and Distributed Throughout the World by

CHARLES C THOMAS • PUBLISHER
2600 South First Street
Springfield, Illinois 62794-9265

© *1993 by* CHARLES C THOMAS • PUBLISHER

ISBN 0-398-05833-4

Library of Congress Catalog Card Number: 92-34665

With THOMAS BOOKS *careful attention is given to all details of manufacturing
and design. It is the Publisher's desire to present books that are satisfactory as to their
physical qualities and artistic possibilities and appropriate for their particular use.*
THOMAS BOOKS *will be true to those laws of quality that assure a good name
and good will.*

Printed in the United States of America
SC-R-3

Library of Congress Cataloging-in-Publication Data

Shea, Marian Axford.
    Handbook for beginning teachers / by Marian Axford Shea.
      p.   cm.
    Includes bibliographical references and index.
    ISBN 0-398-05833-4
    1. First year teachers—United States—Handbooks, manuals, etc.
I. Title.
LB2844.1.N4S54   1993
371.1'0023—dc20   92-34665
                                                    CIP

*Dedicated, lovingly, to all the teachers
in the Shea and Axford families*

PREFACE

THE CULTURE SHOCK OF
WORKING IN A PUBLIC SCHOOL

Welcome to the world of the pedagogue! Probably no profession you could have chosen would have in store for you more potential satisfactions (or more potential frustrations). You have no doubt chosen this profession because you love young people and children. If you did not, GET OUT NOW and read no further. This quality of concern, as you realize, is a *basic essential.*

You no doubt have come from schools of education where many lofty phrases regarding the influence of the life of a teacher on the lives of others have been etched into your thinking. You no doubt are saturated with lectures on education and filled with the idealism which should exude from every young pedagogue. Your eyes are starry (we hope!) and your mind is filled with the dreams of a future, optimistic and opalescent. Good for you! Except that now you face that first day, or perhaps you've already experienced it, and you abruptly descend from the mountaintop of idealism to be encountered by a teeming group of vivacious teen-agers, and, normally enough, some prove to be helpful, others to be resistant, surly, and obstinate. You had felt that they couldn't react this way with *you.* So now you have waded into the icy waters of realism, and you begin to shiver with the cold and anticipate facing a whole year ahead with a group who hasn't responded in any way as you had planned. Lesson plans on paper don't work as you had expected, and there's a Tim or Jim who proves so impossible that the psychology text which contained all the supposedly neat answers proves futile so far as proving of any use to you is concerned.

Now you've encountered the *real* world of teaching—a world of challenge, of sometimes frustration, but of vitality and stimulation. How to keep ahead of this vocal, vital group? Perhaps the contents of this book, if you're ready for it, might prove helpful. At least, give it a try and see if you have any problems similar to the ones mentioned herein. Happy reading, and may your teaching days be fruitful!

ACKNOWLEDGMENTS

To the many people who have contributed through the years to make it possible for this book to come to fruition, I am deeply indebted.

The loss of my late husband, John, an elementary principal, who added zest and joy to my life, gave me the determination to attempt to carry on and pass along a somewhat unusual educational heritage.

Without insistance from my dear brother, Gordon, long-time school administrator and teacher in California schools, and his wife, Margaret, also a teacher, I could never have gotten my California teaching credential.

The fact that I did complete my teaching requirements and spent twenty-two of my teaching years in a progressive district, Kern County Union High School and Community College District, under forward-looking administrators, makes me grateful to that Board of Education and more particularly to Dr. John Collins, Mr. Theron McCuen, and Dr. James Young.

My background in getting my credential from the Education Departments in my two alma maters, Nebraska Wesleyan University and the University of Southern California, provided substantial undergirding. Then much of the contents of this book arose out of lessons I learned the difficult way through practical classroom experiences and from my cherished students and fellow colleagues. To a brother, Fred, and his wife, who provided financial assistance during difficult school days, I owe much.

Some of the original encouragement for writing came from my longtime friends and former colleagues, Rod and Ethel Wessman.

Along the way, guiding my path toward the final goal were my esteemed, patient editor, Payne Thomas, production manager, William Bried, and their staffs. Numerous professors, far more than I can enumerate but who are listed in the endnotes and bibliographies, provided necessary assistance.

With the invaluable expertise and enthusiasm of my faithful brother, Roger, longtime educator in Graduate Education at Arizona State University, and his helpful wife, Geri, I was able to actually finalize the manuscript. My lifelong mentor and sister, Madge, emeritus instructor from Aurora University, and her husband, Hadley, provided assistance as did my sister, Helen, also a teacher and writer.

Helping me greatly with research were the Tempe librarians, Don Koozer, David Park, and Theresa Riel, and with technical and secretarial help were Peter Kee, Erin Morissey, and Mike Robinson. Not to be forgotten is the daily delivery work of Eric Garn, mailman, who brought good news from my publisher.

Encouragement of those who kept my eye on the goal and were of special help were Frances Cassity, Dorothy Kazacik, Jenny Norton, Bernice and Mike Shea, Nita and Larry Stevens, and Marylyn Zupacich.

Hence the book emanates from a lifelong heritage of an educational background beginning with my dad, a teacher, and most of all, my beloved mother, one who taught the indispensable qualities which she learned from the Master Teacher.

Hence we hope to pass along the mantle of a rich educational heritage to our next generation of pedagogues, as Rita continues to teach in Melbourne, Australia, and Scott on the Pima Indian Reservation.

CONTENTS

HANDBOOK FOR
BEGINNING TEACHERS

Chapter 1

THAT FIRST DAY

Ateacher has to make a choice between whether he wants a student to like him on the first day of school or five to ten years later.

Since many pupils today come from backgrounds of chaotic home conditions in which there is much social disorganization, where some never sit down to eat meals together and where there is often much dissension and discontent, quarreling and personal abuse, pupils as a rule respond to an atmosphere of quiet and calm and of strict discipline within the classroom. This ought not to be a discipline where pupils are intimidated, embarrassed, or subjected to sadistic methods, but it should be a discipline of strict adherence to the regular daily routine where day by day a similar schedule is followed with variations within that routine. Techniques which call for originality and various types of creativity work with "gifted" classes, but with those from socially disadvantaged homes the guidelines of routine procedure are important to establish from the first day.

ESTABLISHING PRECEDENT

The imperative of establishing precedent for the entire school year by getting off to an auspicious beginning on its first day cannot be overemphasized. This is the day which establishes guidelines within the classroom within which students continue working for the rest of the school year. Poorly established precedents of classroom control can cause disorganization with which all in the room will have to continue to live for the remainder of the year. Well-established guidelines on the first day can be of vital importance in facilitating smooth classroom procedure.

Ask any experienced secondary teacher regarding this, and he will re-emphasize the point that often the standards and basic patterns established on that first day are patterns largely followed throughout the subsequent days of the school year. At one time during a second-period class on my first day of school I had many interruptions and labored under some difficulties. That class typed me as a poor disciplinarian,

3

and I struggled all during that year to reestablish with that particular class some type of disciplinarian pattern. In another situation, during about the third week of school I began teaching a class which previously had been taught by a poor disciplinarian who had become discouraged and resigned. It was extremely difficult to attempt to reestablish a pattern of discipline. If I could have begun with the same class on the first day of school in establishing precedents, the guidelines set up on that day would have become automatically accepted as the framework within which the class would work.

MAINTAINING A DIGNIFIED DISTANCE

Many teachers do not realize that it can be a fatal mistake to be overly friendly with students on that first day of school. That is the day when each student as a rule comes in a spirit of being willing to listen until he decides what kind of class it will be. Quiet anticipation and suspense reign. There usually is a determination to succeed, a spirit which you must capture. Students come on that day in their newly-acquired clothes. They have an air of excitement about them, and even the one who is most resistant to the educational process is caught up in the excitement which permeates the air, the excitement of being issued new books, meeting new friends, beginning in a new classroom and making a new beginning. Many of those who have previously failed classes have reenrolled or have begun with a fresh determination a year which they feel will offer them a chance to achieve at least a measure of success. During the first few minutes of the class session, when students are determining what kind of class they have been assigned to, and whether or not the teacher will be an "easy mark" or one with strict standards, the teacher is on the offensive. If, during those initial moments of encountering the student, the teacher can impress upon this one who has come perhaps from a non-academic background, the importance which is placed upon respect for authority, courtesy within the classroom, and good grooming, and the extreme importance which the teacher places upon the student's doing his homework and carrying through on assignments, along with the fact that the teacher expects these things to be done, with no nonsense involved, the teacher is off to a propitious start which will no doubt mean a year of good rapport with the students.

OVER-PLAYING STRICTNESS

On that first day the teacher must overplay the fact of strict discipline. It may even be necessary to evict one unruly student from the room and deal with him later in the counselor's office as an example to the others that there will be no countenancing of refractory behavior. If the students understand this from the inception of the course, they as a rule will conform to the standards set. However, usually if the teacher comes well-prepared and immediately captures their interest, this is the best technique for getting students to respond. There are the occasions, though, when that one individual who is noted for making lives of teachers miserable, will attempt to disrupt any move you may make toward class control. This individual must be immediately dealt with *the first time,* and this may avoid many subsequent problems of discipline which will otherwise arise if this individual is ignored. His removal will have immediate quieting effects upon the remainder of the class, and if he is readmitted rather than transferred to another class, I would predict that upon his reentrance to your class he will come with his attitude altered.

STRICTNESS, YET FAIRNESS

Do not worry about the fact that pupils will feel that you are too strict. It is if one is unfair that they will dislike and resent a person. Over the period of the year or years, they will come to understand and know you, but if you are categorized by the students on the first day as an "easy mark," you are off to a year in which you will be constantly on the defensive with them, and you will find yourself among the defeated and unhappy. If they, on the other hand, decide that you are competent and in control of any situation and that they are expected to conform to high standards, you will be successfully launched on a year in which you will be treated with the respect and deference with which you should be treated because of your experience and background. It is to this kind of parent and teacher that a teenager will bring his problems and not to one who immaturely tries to identify with the teenagers themselves.

Perhaps you think that after hearing the standards and expectations which are set up by you on the first day that pupils will rush to their counselor and ask to be removed from your class. This may actually happen, but it is not a bad result. Certainly the ones who remain will be the better pupils.

Usually, whether fortunately or not, however, it is the strict disciplinarian and the teacher whose standards are held high who cannot get students to transfer from his class. Students like the strict teacher, respect him for his consistency and integrity, and, strangely enough, ask that they might again have that teacher for their next school year.

Chapter 2

THAT FIRST DAY (CONTINUED)

SUGGESTED PROCEDURES FOR THE FIRST DAY

The following is suggested classroom procedure for that first day of school. Perhaps it will prove helpful.

A. Get the students seated. (If possible, have a seating chart made out in advance.)

Obviously it is confusing for students to come into the classroom and find their seats. It is helpful if the teacher can get the list in advance of students who will be in the class. Then I usually have them seated alphabetically as I call off their names and assign them seats which can be changed later if necessary. If one can then have them sign a sheet for each row and have someone make out a seating chart, it puts one at an advantage if you can immediately look at a student and call him or her by name. If it is a responsible class I sometimes have them write their name in large letters and turn the sheet of paper *toward* the teacher. (Sometimes this does not work if students are not responsible ones as they will switch the papers or tear them.)

B. Introductions. Introduction of the pupil.

I then suggest that the students ON PAPER introduce themselves to me, suggesting things they might want to include. Paper and pencils will necessarily have to be furnished to those who have not come prepared to write.

A suggested list which you might want to list on the blackboard to help pupils introduce themselves would be:

Their names and address; names of parents or guardians; where one's father or mother works; number or names of brothers and sisters; school they attended last year; courses they are taking in high school; any special problems which the teacher should know.

The last point gives the pupil the opportunity to let the teacher know if a person might have epilepsy, might need to sit closer toward the front of the room to see the blackboard, might have hearing difficulties, or similar situations.

Avoid oral introductions as they often result in loud laughter, ridicule, or chaos. Since many of the young people may come from broken homes, they are often embarrassed to tell of their families or of the fact that their father is dead or that their mother is supporting the family. Many you will find will be living with guardians or others will be in situations where there are second or third marriages.

Introduction of the teacher — The student as a rule is curious to know about his new teacher and wonders what he/she will be like, so this is the teacher's opportunity to tell of his background, of education and experience and this will often command respect and establish status. I usually tell the class where I attended college, where I took graduate work, what professional organizations I belong to within my teaching field, articles I may have written, and how many years I have worked with teenagers in the profession of teaching.

Introduction to the year's course is the next presentation to be made. Here I attempt to grasp the opportunity of capturing the student's interest in the subject, and I present some of the exciting things which I feel are in store for them in the year ahead. I present in as interesting a way as possible the type of material which the textbook will be presenting. In my particular subject I suggest the interest to be found in current short stories, in moving drama, in the literature which people have loved through the ages, and of the attractive format of their textbooks. In other words, I try to do a selling job in the best way I know how to capture their interest and motivate them in wanting to delve into the material of the course. I may suggest or show them projects which exhibits the unusually beautiful work which my former students have done. I might tell them how material will be presented through reading, through panel discussion, through speakers, through TV and films, through current magazines, and through a variety of approaches. I attempt to use my best salesmanship methods to make them know that the year ahead will be jam-packed with interest for them. Notice that on this first day I at no time give them opportunities for oral response; these things come later in the course when they have their opportunity for oral expression.

C. **Going over the school rules and regulations comes next.**

Explanation is necessary, then, that to accomplish these purposes and to achieve the aims before us, there are certain established regulations which are necessary when large groups of people work together. At the time of introductions I often point out the many people who have focused attention upon the opening day of school and made it possible—the parents, the principals and administrators, the board of education, the bus drivers, the custodial help, the teachers, the students themselves. Then I suggest that the taxpayers pay for each day they are there and that because of this we are in a situation of accountability and it would be much different in an informal situation. I emphasize that this is a business in which there is the responsibility incumbent upon all to produce to the utmost of our abilities although we shall have joys and satisfactions in the so doing.

D. Reading the student handbook.

Next it is important to either hand out student handbooks or go over certain regulations which are stated within the student handbook suggesting that this may avoid confusion and heartache which might come later in the year if the student is not cognizant of what the handbook contains. It will avoid much "I didn't know the rule" or "Nobody ever told me" later on.

Although the soul of the beginning teacher may revolt at the pedantry of listing the following rules, the experienced teacher will know that explaining the following will expedite class procedure and avoid much explanation and confusion at a later date.

So—tell the class that:

1. One expects courtesy from the student from the time he enters your classroom door.

2. He is to be *in his seat* by the time the bell rings if he is to be counted present. If it is necessary to be tardy, he is to see you about it *after class.*

3. Pencils are to be sharpened *before* and *after* class. (Perhaps the teacher wants to establish that all classwork writing be in ink.) The point of bringing materials to class seems an obvious one, but I have known students who flunked classes because they constantly forgot to bring materials. For these groups teachers may even need to supply pencils or books at the beginning of the period (A pupil without either of these is invariably a potential problem). A great deal of subsequent confusion can be eliminated if it can be clearly established on the first day that the students must come prepared each day with pen or pencil, books, and materials. (I give a pupil an "F" for the day later on if he does not have materials, and I make this clear on the first day.)

If it is a particularly irresponsible group of pupils, one may have to leave the texts in the room and pass them out at the beginning of each day's session.

A great deal of poor discipline in high school results when a pupil sits through a class without a book. Stress very clearly the point that you will not allow exceptions and that they must bring books each day. At the beginning of each period be sure each of your pupils has a book or that any students who are there without materials should be temporarily sent out—to the library or to do homework elsewhere. One boy without a book can badly upset the total group. A minor point which is helpful is that books should be covered and their names plus the teacher's name and room number could be put on each book. (One large high school in California reported that they cut expenses for lost or damaged books in half the year when they insisted that each one cover his books.) Explain here that books are to be kept clean, that there will be fines for mutilation, and that lost books must be paid for.

4. Desks are to be kept clean, and there is to be no writing on desks. Here again I explain how I realize how easy it is to "doodle," but if they doodle be sure it is on paper and not on the desk. I stress that there will be fines for writing on desks. Then I charge these fines the minute I find a mark on any desk. It is interesting how quickly this deters other's mutilation of property. One charge of 50¢ or $1.00 on the first few days will avoid a great deal of mutilation of property later on. Also I write on the blackboard, "Anyone writing on a desk will be fined." It has been interesting through the years to notice that when I look at that sign (which irks me) and decide to erase it and treat pupils in a more mature manner, I begin immediately to find marks on desks.

5. Students are not to ask to leave the room during the period unless they have an excuse from their parents or the office, or unless there is some emergency. Rest room breaks are to be taken *between* periods.

Here is a rule which it took me some years to learn is as important as it is, which must be enforced. As a young teacher, I learned the hard way by discovering that someone whom I had let go during the period was found smoking in the restroom or that a high school boy would have a rendezvous with his girl friend when I had thought he had gone on an errand.

Also checking of attendance is vitally important each day. The attendance office competence is the secret to much of a school's efficiency.

6. Students are not to be readmitted to class without a permit from the office.

Most administrations stress the importance of good attendance checking. Any teacher who has taught for long realizes the importance of strict checking, particularly with students whose habits are irregular. Only a new teacher fails to realize how often students may forge passes or attempt to get out of class for various reasons. If any student is absent from your class, BE SURE that at the beginning of the next day you have a valid excuse through parents or through the office. If a teacher is not cognizant of the whereabouts of the pupil, he may be on the streets downtown, peddling dope around the corner, smoking, or getting into any of a variety of kinds of trouble. Delinquency often begins with absenteeism. It is the teacher's responsibility to communicate to the pupil how important it is to maintain regular attendance.

Tardies, too, must be carefully checked. In some secondary schools, after six tardies the pupil is dropped from the class. Other teachers maintain that three tardies without excuse will bring the grade down one point. When pupils realize that the reason for strict tardy checking is to enable them later to hold good jobs, they will respect this point. The teacher who checks carefully after class for the reason for the tardy will know that this is important for the same reason as careful attendance checking.

7. The student is expected to turn in his homework *regularly* and *on time.* I explain that I do not accept late homework. There is always some important exception, of course, but as a basic rule I have found that if the pupils learn that they must meet the requirement deadline, they will plan their work accordingly. Otherwise one will run into difficulty in accepting late papers. I explain that for an absence he will have as many days to make up his work as he was absent.

There may be other rules important to the smooth functioning of class procedure throughout the year which have not been included in the above. Each teacher will want to add his own and the pupils may have some to suggest.

It is unfortunate that the working together of so many hundreds of young people requires many rules and regulations. The larger the school, obviously, the more complex the structure and the more rules and regulations to make life easier. I try to point out that these rules are means towards an end of the "greatest good to the greatest number" of people, that working in a public school situation is vastly different from having the opportunity of a person-to-person relationship such as in a tutoring situation or a private school setup. I also try to point out that when students themselves are involved in rule-making, such as in their student council group, these are the same rules as those which usually evolve from such a group. Then I proceed one step further attempting to point out that when we learn to adjust to these basic guidelines, life becomes easier for all. Rules and regulations, then, are to facilitate working together and not to make life more difficult.

Life will be made far easier for all for the entire year if regulations are clarified and understood by all from the very first day.

QUESTIONS

1. What is meant by "establishing precedent" on the first day of school? What difference does it make how the first day goes?
2. Why is it important to maintain a dignified distance with one's students? What kinds of problems might be created if one doesn't?
3. List a few procedures which might be followed on that first day of school in helping to make the year easier throughout the remaining weeks. Why might it be helpful for students to participate in setting these suggested standards?

Chapter 3

HOW TO GET GOOD DISCIPLINE

The problem of maintaining good discipline in the classroom is one which is faced by all teachers. Probably the inability to maintain discipline has been the cause of more people's quitting the teaching profession, and of their disillusionment and heartbreak regarding what teaching would entail, than any other cause.

It is almost impossible to tell another person how to maintain good discipline within the classroom; this is something which each teacher handles differently, and when problem situations arise, people solve those problems according to their own particular methods and differently at different times and with individual students. However, there are certain basic guidelines regarding the maintenance of respect and order which definitely can be followed and certain suggestions which I feel any instructor would agree make for good discipline within a teaching situation.

The following are suggestions which should definitely aid the beginning teacher in maintaining discipline:

1. BE MORE THAN ADEQUATELY PREPARED

The top-flight athletes call it "overtrain." Adequate preparation of the teacher can insure good discipline more than any other one thing. If the teacher is well-organized and has his/her material well in hand, knows exactly what he will be assigning and can communicate to the class his own organization and preparation, this will immediately insure confidence within his students. It will also give the teacher himself the feeling of being on the *offensive* instead of on the defensive in dealing with student problems.

2. NAMES ARE IMPORTANT

Have your name either written on the board or where students can see it. Also have a seating chart made out in advance so that when the students enter the classroom you immediately call each by the first name. Sometimes this cannot be possible until seats are assigned or until the second day, but there is nothing which commands the student's attention and lets him know you are in control as much as immediately calling him by name. Seating arrangement and seat assignment is important, for often just changing someone's seat can solve a problem.

3. MAKE THE CLASS INTERESTING, AND VARY ACTIVITIES

If a variety of media can be used in presenting lesson materials—special speakers, films, writing, reading, reports—and the student is insured of the fact that each day he comes there will be something which will capture his interest, he will come to the class with an expectant attitude and can be confident that there will be something of interest in store for him.

4. KNOWING THE "ATTENTION SPAN" OF STUDENTS IS EXTREMELY IMPORTANT

For the reason that more mature students have longer "attention spans" than do immature or slower learners, it is vitally important for a teacher to note the "attention span" of different classes and different pupils and change activities accordingly. Grouping is important because some students can maintain much longer interest than others, and as students mature they can concentrate for a longer period of time.

5. BE IN THE CLASSROOM EARLY

Always be in the classroom before any student arrives. By the time the student enters, the teacher should be fully equipped to know exactly what will be happening essentially within the classroom that day. Sometimes it is well to keep students outside the room until all preparations for them have been adequately made. However, some problems may arise if students have to wait, so it is best if the teacher can, as a rule, be there and prepared before any students come. If you need to move from room to room, try to have materials on the desk, assignment on the board, and everything ready to begin before students are allowed to enter. Then they usually will enter in a different atmosphere and with a different manner than if you are unprepared.

6. HAVE A NEAT CLASSROOM

If papers from a former class are on the floor as students enter, the students are much more apt to assume a lack of discipline exists.

7. HAVE OUTLINES AND ASSIGNMENTS TO BE DISTRIBUTED READY IN ADVANCE

This, again, puts one on the *offensive* rather than on the defensive. If, when the pupils come into a classroom, they are given an assignment sheet at the beginning of class it will capture their attention, or, if you are planning to show a film, if the film is set up and ready to be shown, they will usually respond in a spirit of readiness. Be sure you have their attention before you begin the class. If you are showing a film, turn on the lights before the room is darkened for showing the film and make it understood that you expect the attention of the whole group before you proceed and sometimes you may even have them take notes.

8. GET THE CLASS STARTED

In maintaining good discipline, it is important to start the class immediately. Even if you give a five-minute assignment for them to reread some particular paragraphs, or even if you have some reliable student take the attendance for you if attendance slips must go to the office at the beginning of classes, GET THE CLASS STARTED. This will make the time for tardies a definite time. If you are not consistent as to the exact time for tardies, this can cause much class disruption and run into difficulties. If you are responsible for taking attendance, you can do it either while the class is reading or while a student is reciting, but if you START ON TIME, you will not have to attempt to reestablish discipline and there will not be time for difficulties to develop. Students with questions or problems can be called up to you later in the period, after class, or later can arrange time for a conference.

If you start the class immediately, the class will, as a rule, automatically become quiet and respectful. If, on the other hand, you, for some reason, are forced to be detained, students will begin talking, giggling, joking, and it will be difficult to recapture their attention.

This is a harder rule to follow than it may appear to be. Many things will happen to tempt you to break it. In some schools attendance records must be turned in within the first five or ten minutes. Nevertheless, if one can always adhere to the principle of beginning the class on time, much difficulty will be avoided. This rule holds for EACH DAY.

9. PRECEDENT FOR DISCIPLINE IS
SET ON THE FIRST DAY

Begin the year by confronting the class with a dignified, serious manner. Your demeanor should portray confidence and strength of authority, with an interest in the situation which stresses the great importance of this vibrant moment of starting school and launching upon a year which will be of vital import to teachers and pupils alike. YOU CANNOT BE TOO STRICT ON THE FIRST DAY SO LONG AS YOU ARE FAIR. Do NOT try on that first day to be one of the group, but maintain a respectful distance.

10. SPOT THE TROUBLEMAKER

There may be one or two troublemakers in each class. If you can, at the outset, pinpoint the one or two troublemakers and never give them an opportunity to upset the class, you will begin and maintain a decorum throughout the year. Sometimes it is more difficult than you may think to determine who is the troublemaker. He may fool you, and it may even be one who is seemingly quiet or cooperative who is upsetting others, but through the other pupils who react, you will soon find out. If, within the first day or two you can isolate the troublemaker, either by removing him from the room and calling him in later for a counselor or parent conference, the quieting effect upon him and upon the rest of the class will be felt, and you will have communicated to the class the idea that class control is maintained and that the expectation is for that class control to be the norm.

When a teacher finds it necessary to be absent, it is always good to leave for the substitute teacher a seating chart, pinpointing the names of two or three people in the class who should be watched. This, many times, facilitates the work of the substitute more than any other one thing.

11. BE SURE THAT EVERYONE HAS SOMETHING TO DO

If you can immediately spot the person who is through with his work or who needs an additional assignment or attention, you can deal individually with his situation. Be sure that each student has come prepared with a book and materials or in some cases you may need to furnish a book or pen. If you can keep each one busy, you will avoid discipline trouble.

12. GOOD GROOMING COMMANDS RESPECT

Good grooming on the part of the teacher is important. A teacher's attitude of poise and security is contagious; also he/she has more self-esteem if well dressed.

13. WHAT YOU DO SPEAKS LOUDER THAN WHAT YOU SAY

Since students learn by imitation and example, your actions and speech are what is important. If you are working at correcting papers or if you are busily engaged, often pupils will tend to imitate your involvement. A quiet, consistent, interested attitude will inspire the same in pupils. Maintaining one's own stability is the greatest asset for a teacher in keeping control.

14. BE CONSISTENT

You cannot have certain regulations one day and then change drastically the next. Therefore, it is important to set up guidelines at the outset, and, while exceptions always have to be made, if the pupils understand definitely the framework within which they should work, as a rule they will respect and abide by those guidelines.

15. AVOID HAVING DEAD TIME

Dead time is a major contributor to classroom control problems. Dead time is created when students sit idly waiting for the teacher to write something on the board or to begin the class. It is created when students wait for the teacher to help them. It also is created when instructional time is used inappropriately. When a teacher stops the whole class to give directions to a few or to tell the class that they're getting too noisy, it makes for discipline problems. Dead time results when teachers play an overly dominant role which does not allow students to make decisions and act independently.[1]

After the rules are understood and clarified (and often the pupils themselves can help determine what they should be), then one can proceed positively. Obviously, pupils respond most favorably to praise and recognition. After high standards have been established and they know they are expected to meet stringent requirements, they can produce work in which they take great pride. Individual recognition of their accomplishments and kind words of praise are most welcome to them, and they respond positively when given both. They will as a rule go to great lengths to please their teacher or to gain the recognition of their peers.

ENDNOTES

1. Shepardson, Richard D., *Elementary Teacher's Discipline Desk Book,* West Nyack, Parker Publishing, 1980, p. 33.

QUESTIONS

1. How can a teacher's preparation be compared to an athlete's "over-training"?
2. Why is it important to learn students' names as soon as possible and what has this to do with discipline?
3. What kinds of things can be done so that the class will not be boring?
4. What do we mean by "attention span," and how does this relate to maintaining discipline?
5. What advantage does a teacher have who arrives early?
6. Explain the function neatness plays.
7. What is the advantage of having an assignment sheet ready for the students?
8. Comment on why a teacher should start the class on time.
9. Can a teacher be too strict on the first day of school? With what must the strictness be tempered?
10. How should one deal with the troublemaker?
11. Why is it important to be sure each one in the class either has brought his/her materials or for the teacher to furnish such?
12. What role does grooming play?

Chapter 4

WHEN SHOULD YOU
INTERCEDE TO DISCIPLINE?

Teachers who have discipline problems are sometimes guilty of overreacting to minor incidents. They may nail students for minor errors or, on the other hand, they may not see the first offender and then accuse the wrong person.

Here are some basic principles:

1. As a rule, trust your students.

Believe in your students and don't treat them like enemies. Give them enough time to make mistakes and then enough time to correct their errors.[1]

2. Keep your educational objectives in mind, and keep things in perspective. A sign of professional maturity is the ability to judge the severity of an act and to act accordingly.

3. Remember that you're not the only reinforcing agent in the classroom.

Other students in the classroom may also be reinforcing agents. If others are involved in the misbehavior, direct your remarks at all those involved.

When should you intercede? You should intercede if:

a. The misbehavior threatens anyone's health or well-being.
b. Other students begin to join in or encourage the offender.
c. The misbehavior is distracting other students and interfering with your instructional program.
d. The offender is not meeting a behavior commitment that was made previously.
e. The misbehavior is interfering with other classes or could lead to public relations problems with parents or staff.
f. Other students observed the misbehavior and are looking at you, waiting to see what you are going to do.

If you have to intercede, your reaction should reflect the severity of the act. If at all possible, postpone any direct confrontation with the student until after the lesson or until you can do so privately.[2]

4. **Probe the reasons; don't pass premature judgment.** Give yourself time to see what's happening, and be slow to pass judgment. If your students sense your faith in them, they will many times react by fulfilling your expectations.[3]

5. **Avoid public win/lose confrontations.**

When you confront a student publicly, you run a great risk of losing face with your students. In almost all audience situations, the teacher will come out the loser. If you come down hard on a child or punish the student in front of the class, some students are going to see you as being unfair or too harsh. On the other hand, others will see you as being too soft, or an easy mark. Few will look at you as being fair. Even if they do, your action will have negative ripple effects. Other students will indirectly feel threatened and feel they may be next.[4]

6. **Don't embarrass students or make them lose face in front of their classmates.**

If you try to coerce, you should provide a way for the student to save face without forcing a win/lose confrontation.[5]

7. **Concentrate on the behavior and not on the child.**

Teachers who are specific in their reactions get more conformity to class standards and have fewer class disruptions when compared to teachers who are general and don't give reasons for their reactions.

8. **State exactly why the behavior is inappropriate and why it is so.**

9. **Use humor to acknowledge a "would be" problem.**

A little humor can be effective in turning a "would be" discipline case into a lighthearted situation. In that way sometimes the message can be communicated without a confrontation or unpleasant scene.[6]

Control Theory: Student Needs and Possible Solutions

THE NEED TO BELONG

- create a classroom with an accepting atmosphere
- create a sense of ownership
- recognize a students' attempts to be accepted
- praise students' performances (athletic, choral, journalistic, etc.)
- teach using groups; use cooperative learning strategies
- discipline or reprimand in private whenever possible; avoid humiliating students

THE NEED FOR FREEDOM

- involve students in rulemaking
- provide opportunities for free expression
- encourage creativity in assignments
- consider eliminating assigned seating (with consequences, of course)

THE NEED FOR POWER

- share leadership responsibilities
- display students' work on bulletin boards, on walls, on clotheslines, etc.
- use praise at every opportunity
- afford students opportunities to talk and/or to teach
- encourage the success of every student
- create a student-centered classroom
- give students choices any time there is an opportunity (theme topics, test questions, projects, seating arrangement, curriculum planning)

THE NEED FOR FUN

- encourage students to have a good time learning
- use games and simulations
- create a classroom that is a "fun place to be"
- use humor whenever appropriate
- display willingness to laugh at yourself
- teach as though learning is to be enjoyed[1]

ENDNOTES

1. Shepardson, Richard D., *Elementary Teacher's Discipline Desk Book*, West Nyack, Parker, 1980, pp. 188–190.
2. *Ibid.*, p. 190.
3 and 4. *Ibid.*, p. 194.
5. *Ibid.*, p. 194.
6. *Ibid.*, pp. 196–197.

---

[1]Farris, R.S., "Meeting Their Needs in Motivating . . . Learners" *Middle School Journal*, Vol. 22, #2, Nov. 1990, p. 24.

QUESTIONS

1. What type of attitude should a teacher consistently maintain which helps with discipline?
2. What is meant by having other reinforcing agents?
3. List some times when a teacher should intercede to enforce discipline.
4. Into what difficulty does one run if he/she confronts the pupil publicly?
5. If it seems absolutely necessary to use coercion, what should one provide?
6. Comment regarding being specific.
7. How can humor sometimes alleviate a difficult situation?

Chapter 5

PHYSICAL NEEDS OF PUPILS

A variety of physical needs could be listed, any list of which would be far from complete. Each teacher can compile a list of his own, but there will be many physical problems encountered, each differing according to the particular situation.

1. EYESIGHT PROBLEMS

Almost all schools recognize the importance of conducting eye tests for individual pupils and recording the results on the cumulative record folder. Beginning in the primary grades, it is important to spot a pupil who has eye difficulties. These difficulties, of course, can result in many emotional and psychological problems as well. Many pupils have had reading difficulties which result from inability to see the printed page. It is important at the first of the school year to recognize which pupils need attention in this regard, those who need to be seated near the front of the room in order to see well, those who need to have other activities rather than to be subjected to too much eye strain.

The *dyslexic* pupil is one who exhibits poor ability to discriminate visual images or transposes letters within a word.

William Mulligan, Chief Probation Officer for Sonoma County, California, and chairman of the committees on the Neurologically Handicapped Children and for the Chief Probation Officers' Association, has made a study of a total case load of sixty juveniles to determine chronological age, grade placement, and reading level. The study was made because of the awareness that such a large number of children referred to his department for delinquent tendencies were reading below grade level.

While Mr. Mulligan does not maintain that dyslexia is the cause for delinquency, he found some within the group studied who were dyslexic and feels that dyslexia is a contributing factor in delinquency. He defines dyslexia as "the defective language achievement in an individual who has normal intelligence and normal achievement in all other areas of learning. Language involves talking, reading, writing, spelling, and speech, and one or all of these may be affected in a dyslexic child."[1]

The purpose of our inclusion of this study here is that the teacher might recognize tendencies in this direction before the problem has developed and be able to refer the individual for counseling, tutoring, or for additional help before his problem becomes acute.

Probation Officer Mulligan continues to point out that because of a child's inability to achieve in the regular school setting, as he progresses through school, he realizes he is falling farther and farther behind the other pupils. When he is placed in the slower groups, his image of himself is damaged and with the consequence that he may either withdraw and not enter into the class work or he will attempt to act out in class or in his other environment; sometimes he will feign illness rather than to continue in a situation where he continually fails.[2]

How would a teacher recognize a dyslexic pupil? Marion Fenwick Stuart has pointed out several symptoms: (1) Poor ability to discriminate visual likenesses or differences in words; (2) Poor ability in visual recall of words even though he has studied them well; (3) Poor ability to discriminate between close gradation of sound even though hearing is normal; (4) Poor ability to recall whole sounds or sounds within words; (5) Poor ability to associate spoken letter sounds or words with the corresponding visual symbols; (6) Directional confusions; (7) Ambidexterity in that uncertainty as to which hand to use is a common hesitancy; (8) Tendency toward motor clumsiness. She also lists others such as poor ability to reproduce rhythm as sequences, dysfunctions in relationships, speech or language disorders, and behavior problems such as hyperactivity and distractibility.

William Mulligan as a probation officer points out that children who exhibit dyslexic tendencies should not be compelled to attend classes in which they face competition and daily frustration but that the teacher should learn to identify these pupils and recommend them for special attention and treatment.

A teacher, then, if she notes that a pupil makes errors such as writing "three" as "there," "shop" for "hope," "mane" for "name" *consistently* over periods of time or that he has difficulty in discriminating so far as recalling whole words or sounds, should be alert to the *possibility* that he may be a dyslexic and need referral for special help and attention.

2. HEARING DIFFICULTIES

Even as an instructor should be alert to eye problems, likewise hearing difficulties might be the cause of many academic problems. Usually one can recognize one with a hearing problem by his listlessness or in-attention or even the expression on his face when one addresses a question to him. The best way, of course, is to know the results of the hearing tests which have been conducted and then one can be accurate regarding how much loss of hearing one has. Obviously, these students need to be placed where the good ear can pick up the best sounds or close to the speaker. Don't be fooled, however, as I once was, when I began teaching, when a boy had in his ear something which I mistook for a hearing aid and soon discovered was a transistor radio, and he was listening to the current World Series ball games!

3. SPEECH DIFFICULTIES

Some schools have special instructors or special classes which are conducted for those with speech difficulties. Those difficulties might be lisping, stuttering, or other maladies. The stutterer, of course, should never be pressured or hurried but should be given reassurance and supportiveness, and sometimes with proper understanding and encouragement his handicap can be largely overcome.

While language difficulties cannot be classified as physical handicaps, they can present a handicap in an academic situation. Thus young people from bi-lingual backgrounds or from backgrounds in which they have had different speech patterns from the one accepted by their peer group need to have additional encouragement and understanding. Shameless accounts of violence done to personalities can be related regarding embarrassment because of language different from that spoken within a classroom. Actually the bi-lingual student should be made to feel proud of his heritage. A "white, upper-middle-class" instructor should learn that in dealing with some groups of Latin American or other cultures the pace is far slower than the pace of North Americans. If instructors have in their class Mexican-Americans, for example, many times it will take them almost five minutes to decide to open a book, to recite, or to respond, and some instructors find this irritating. Perhaps we could learn some things from their more relaxed culture. Some black pupils may be entirely differently oriented to time than white pupils and five to fifteen minutes difference might not have the same meaning at all to them. Some of them are taught that it is rude to look into the face of one in authority, that they should stand before them with eyes downcast, whereas the "white, upper-middle-class" instructor will feel that it is a sign of the student's being recalcitrant for him to react in such a manner. It is most important to learn why the pupils have certain patterns of behavior.

4. PROBLEMS OF EPILEPSY

Usually the student, his parents, or the administration will inform one if there is one in the classroom who has problems of epilepsy. There are many varieties of epilepsy, ranging from petit mal, which is characterized by mild convulsive seizure with transient clouding of consciousness to grand mal, which is severe epilepsy. Fortunately, epilepsy now can be many times kept under control by medication. However, in case of a pupil's experiencing a seizure within a classroom situation, it is important for the one in charge to know that the main requirement is to keep the rest of the class calm and away from the victim of the seizure, to loosen his clothing and perhaps to put a pencil between his teeth to keep him from biting his tongue but other than that to let the seizure run its course, or of course one can send immediately for the school nurse by sending someone to call her. Probably it is as important to keep the class from panicking as anything, and this can be utilized as an educational situation in which the students can learn that epilepsy has been something which has been surrounded by much misunderstanding and superstition. It should not take long for the victim to recover, and a calm and intelligent instructor can skillfully handle what might otherwise be a troublesome situation. It is also important for that instructor to know if a child has mild attacks which might not be evidenced to the class but which might explain why that child might at times exhibit aberrant behavior.

5. PROBLEMS OF DIABETES

If a young person has told the teacher that he is a diabetic, it might be that from time to time he needs to leave the room in order to take medicine or because of unusual thirst. It is well for a teacher to be cognizant of this problem.

6. PROBLEMS OF HOMOSEXUALITY, OF KLEPTOMANIA, OF HYPERTENSION, OF HYPOTENSION

Probably the list is inexhaustible of types of problems which one might encounter, and the best way to know of these problems is to study the previous records kept on a pupil. It is well to know that if a pupil might be a homosexual he might fall into fits of depression or feel badly rejected; if he is one with kleptomaniac tendencies, he will want to take money or valuables which belong to others, for no apparent reason, not for need but only for the thrill he might experience in being able to take material things. A person with hypertensive tendencies might be extremely "high-strung" or nervous, whereas one who has hypotensive tendencies would be quite the opposite.

One is fortunate if he finds himself in a school situation where there are specialists employed to work with pupils who are physically or otherwise handicapped, but this is not always the case. A background of understanding of the problems and handicaps of students can do much and go far in helping them avoid frustrations, sorrows, and difficulties. Hopefully the school's knowledge of their difficulties and an intelligent procedure in dealing with those difficulties will go far in changing the direction of their lives and assisting them in becoming worthwhile and constructive citizens.

QUESTIONS

1. What is meant by the "dyslexic" pupil?
2. How could a teacher recognize a "dyslexic" pupil?
3. How is the best way for a teacher to be cognizant of the fact that a pupil may have a hearing problem?
4. How can teachers from different cultural backgrounds learn to adjust to pupils of various types of backgrounds?
5. What is it best to remember in dealing with either a health crisis in the classroom or any other unexpected occurrence?
6. Why is it helpful to study the cumulative records regarding those with whom one deals and what are some unexpected problems which might be recorded there?

Chapter 6

EMOTIONAL AND PSYCHOLOGICAL
NEEDS OF PUPILS

To be an alert and effective instructor, it is important to be able to recognize the *tendencies* of pupils in directions of certain emotional and psychological problems. This does not mean that one immediately categorizes each pupil as a psychological case, but it does mean that the alert teacher is cognizant of the fact that tendencies toward certain emotional and psychological problems in pupils do exist and that it is his responsibility to be able to deal with these problems so far as recognition of them is concerned. Many times students have an inability to learn the meanings of abstractions on a printed page because they have difficulties which prevent them from concentrating or learning.

In this section, only some of the difficulties of pupils will be dealt with and those only in so far as they need to be recognized by the teacher, not necessarily dealt with. Many times it is the responsibility of the teacher who recognizes difficulty to talk with the parent, to refer the pupil to a counselor or to a clinic. The teacher's responsibility lies in the area of being aware of pupil difficulties.

Only a few categories will be dealt with here, and the teacher in training can refer further to books of psychology dealing with other disorders. It is well, however, for him to be able to recognize some of these basic patterns in an effort to ward off more severe psychological problems. Every classroom may have individuals who have *tendencies* in the direction of problems listed.

1. THE ATTENTION-GETTER

Probably this type of individual is the one who will be most upsetting to the beginning teacher. Many times this type of behavior is resultant from lack of attention in a home situation. Various means will be used to get the class's or the teacher's attention. This is indicative of severe emotional need on the part of the pupil and many times this individual can be dealt with by giving him additional responsibility in aiding others in the class or in helping the teacher organize activities.

2. THE WITHDRAWN INDIVIDUAL

Psychological studies have shown that in observing control groups of monkeys which were raised in group-living situations and comparing them with monkeys raised in motherless group situations, the "deprived" monkeys who had experienced little concern or mothering, sat passively in their cages and stared vacantly into space, paying little attention to the monkeys in neighboring cages or to the activities of workers in the room.[1] This type of behavior has also been noted in severely withdrawn patients in mental institutions. Thus, if in a classroom a pupil exhibits *abnormally* withdrawn or antisocial behavior, it might be concluded that he has been deprived of "normal" mothering or concern within a home situation. Also the individual who *excessively* daydreams might in later life experience psychological difficulties as do mental patients who find they cannot deal with reality, who live in a world of unrealism, and who cannot tackle problems in real situations. *Tendencies* in these directions should be dealt with by the intelligent teacher, by a stress on not procrastinating, on facing reality, and on tackling tasks assigned. Be sure to distinguish between one with creative imagination and one who is aimlessly daydreaming as a regular habit. This one cannot always do, certainly. Schizophrenic tendencies, however, should be noted early.

3. TENDENCIES TOWARD DEMENTIA PRAECOX

Similar to the above, or closely connected, are tendencies toward dementia praecox, a loss or impairment of mental powers. This usually begins in late adolescence, and is characterized by melancholia, withdrawal, hallucinations, delusions, etc.

4. DELUSIONS OF GRANDEUR

Delusions, of course, implies belief in something that is contrary to fact or reality. Pupils can delude themselves or others or exaggerate stories to the point that they actually believe things not real. Such things as rationalizing or lying can begin to evidence themselves and if allowed to persist can lead to real psychological and mental difficulties.

5. PARANOIA

The mental disorder of paranoia is characterized by delusions also, but especially of persecution. This type of student we say "has a chip on his shoulder." He may feel that he is being excessively persecuted or he may interpret many actions toward him as persecution and we sometimes say he has a "persecution complex." If a teacher recognizes this tendency or trait in a pupil, the teacher will deal with it objectively and not take any statements or derogatory epithets or profane language toward him as anything personal. He will recognize it for what it is, a personality difficulty in the student himself.

6. MANIC DEPRESSION

A person with a tendency in this direction is characterized by alternating periods of melancholia, or mental depression. Any tendency toward a mania would be characterized by abnormal excitability or obsession.

7. EXTROVERSION AND INTROVERSION

"Extroversion," as defined by psychologists, refers to the individual who directs his interest to phenomena outside himself rather than to his own experiences and feelings, whereas "introversion" refers to an individual who has a tendency to direct his interest upon himself rather than upon external objects or events.

Other psychological tendencies and difficulties could be listed or noted, but the main emphasis is that a teacher should be alert to *tendencies* toward psychological problems which should be dealt with early in life. Many times if problems are acute or in immediate need of attention, a counselor, a priest or minister, or a physician or guidance person should have the student referred to him and the teacher should not feel that his responsibility extends beyond the point of the recognition of the difficulty and the attempt to deal with the problem objectively and compassionately.

ENDNOTES

1. Halling, Dr. Victor J., *Search for Truth: Studies in Psychology,* Dubuque, Kendall-Hunt, 1961 (From *Journal of Natural History,* December, 1961).

QUESTIONS

1. What is sometimes the problem which makes one an "attention-getter"? How can one deal with this in the classroom?
2. What may have been in the background of the "withdrawn" individual which makes him/her as he/she is? Is there a danger if a pupil daydreams excessively?
3. To what can excessive melancholia lead? Excessive rationalizing or lying? Excessive feelings of being persecuted?
4. How involved should a competent teacher get in such situations, or to what extent should the teacher become involved?
5. What are some positive courses of action which a teacher might pursue in helping individual pupils?

Chapter 7

UNDERSTANDING THE DROP-OUT

CORRELATION BETWEEN READING
AND DROPPING OUT OF SCHOOL

The correlation between inability to read and dropping out of school is very high. A comparison of two groups of students—593 poor readers and 593 good readers—who were enrolled in the Battle Creek, Michigan High School in 1956 in a four-year period showed that more of the poor readers dropped out of school. More specifically, 296, or 49.9 percent, of the poor readers dropped out of school before graduation; whereas only eighty-six, or 14.5 percent, of the good readers dropped out of school before graduation. Statistically, the difference between the percentages of the poor readers and the good readers who dropped out of school before graduation was significant at the .01 level. To look at it in another way, in the same groups of poor readers and good readers, 270, or 45.5 percent, of the poor readers were graduated from high school, whereas 481, or 81.2 percent, of the good readers were graduated from high school.

The peak of school leaving for the *poor* readers occurred during the tenth grade, 120, or 20.2 percent, of the 593 *poor* readers dropped out of school and another thirty-eight, or 12.8 percent, dropped out of school after the completion of the tenth grade. Among the 296 *poor* readers who dropped out of school before graduation, 53.3 percent dropped out of school during or immediately after completing the tenth grade. On the other hand, only eight, or 1.3 percent, of the *good* readers dropped out of school during the tenth grade and an additional thirteen, or 2.2 percent, dropped out of school after the completion of the tenth grade. In other words, more than three times as many poor readers as good readers dropped out of school before graduation.[1]

It would seem logically to follow, then, that if the teacher can help improve the reading ability of the student, the rate of dropout would be greatly lowered.

CORRELATION BETWEEN READING AND DELINQUENCY

Studies have proven that there is a high correlation between dropping out of school and becoming delinquent. Department of Employment personnel people can readily testify to the facts that many in the long line of unemployed are those who have not completed high school. There seems to be a vicious circle between inability to read, discouragement, dropping out of school, being unable to find work, getting into petty theft or involved in minor crimes, going to juvenile hall, and becoming delinquent. Probation officers, too, can cite statistics which verify this correlation.

PROBLEMS DROP-OUTS FACE

Problems which face the drop-out students become many. The drop-out student is limited vocationally because he is usually poorly prepared to take his place in the adult world of work. He can be considered for employment in those jobs only which do not require high school graduation. In the 71 occupations where labor shortages exist, the minimum educational requirement for all 71 is at least four years of schooling at the high school level. The trend is increasingly toward more jobs for the educated and skilled and fewer for the unskilled. Almost everywhere in the United States employers are more reluctant to hire non-high school graduates.[2]

The drop-out is limited economically because he must be satisfied with an earning power which is lower than that commanded by a person with a high school education. Since, for the most part, he will be an unskilled worker with uncertain periods of employment, he will have a fixed income which is usually quite low and often not enough to make ends meet.

The drop-out is also limited *socially* in that he rarely contributes much to society. He must cope with feelings of inferiority and inadequacy brought on by the realization that his friends and neighbors are better educated than he. Since this teen-ager drop-out often becomes a marginal worker or a drifter, with more frequent and longer periods of unemployment than his skilled peers, he will tend to become imbued with a sense of failure or rejection. As a result, he may then join others like himself in acts of resentment against society.[3]

What are the holding power factors and the hastening power factors in the high school drop-out situation? The following factors are considered of primary importance to dropping out of school:

Holding power factors:

1. Out-of-school employment.
2. Participation in extra-curricular activities.
3. Having a sense of belonging in high school.
4. Participation in out-of-school activities.
5. Having school spirit.
6. Good attitude of parents toward education.
7. The pupil's having a career plan.
8. A desire to complete high school.

Hastening power factors:

1. Elementary school failures.
2. Absences in the ninth grade.
3. Low scholastic aptitude.
4. Being a discipline case.

What are the contributing factors of secondary importance?

1. Skilled father in preference to unskilled.
2. Good citizenship rating.
3. Living with both natural parents.

Hastening power factors:

1. High school subject failure.
2. High school absences.
3. Physical defects.

Part of the responsibility for keeping the teenager in school lies with the school itself. To make school work more meaningful and less discouraging to the potential drop-out, the following suggestions are given to improve secondary education:

1. **The curriculum of the high school needs to offer courses adapted to the interests and abilities of the students beginning with the 9th or 10th grades.** Offering a curriculum which is of vital importance to the pupil and which will maintain his interest and challenge his ability is crucial to the problem of prevention of drop-outs.

2. **Improved guidance services.** The potential drop-out needs help with his personal problems, not just when he is "in trouble," but before his problems become critical. It is the responsibility of the alert teacher

to properly and correctly refer the pupil for counseling when it is needed or to anticipate when it is needed. The pupil needs help in realistic self-appraisal and in seeing how each of his in-class experiences helps him reach goals that he accepts. More time is needed for counseling, and counseling services should be extended downward into the elementary grades, as they are in many schools, where many of the school adjustment problems of early school-leavers first become evident. Increased emphasis on counseling is also important at those points where pupils face decisions affecting their continuation in school.

Students likely to end their schooling at high school graduation or before need help in choosing a suitable vocation and the high school subjects that will prepare them for it. They need help in getting pertinent information about a variety of occupations and in assessing their own abilities. Their choices should be made consciously rather than by default, and made with skillful guidance.

3. **Pupil records** can be improved to provide more of the information needed for adequate pupil guidance. School counselors can initiate case conferences and other types of drop-out studies, and they can exchange information directly with teachers. Records should be readily accessible to the teachers and counselors who use them.

4. **Improved classroom opportunities.** Normally the goals of the non-drop-out, derived from his family and friends, his plans for college, or his vocational choice, lead him to want respectable marks and teacher approval. He is therefore likely to accept teacher-assigned tasks relatively uncritically. For the potential drop-out, however, this is not the case. His family and friends may place little value on school. His plans probably do not include college or an occupation he can prepare for in school. School work is probably difficult for him. All in all, it is imperative that his classes meet more immediate needs if he is to continue in school. He must be helped to see the needs which his classes immediately meet.

5. **Grouping pupils according to their abilities** for academic courses makes it easier to meet the needs of the individual. For social purposes he can be in non-grouped classes which are non-academic. The content and teaching methods used in each group must be suited to the needs of the pupils, and those of lower ability should not be stigmatized by their group assignments. If reading is so poor as to handicap pupils in much of their school work, it may be necessary to provide special reading classes.

Better classroom opportunities for the potential drop-out may also be provided by the addition of courses such as those in vocational fields, core or common-learning courses, driver training, and work experience supervised by the school. Merely adding new courses or changing the names of existing subjects will accomplish little. The courses must be meaningful to the potential drop-out.

6. **The potential drop-out needs extracurricular activity in keeping with his interests and abilities.** Many of the extra-curricular activities available in schools are not of particular interest to the potential drop-out. Others make demands for successful performance that are beyond his abilities. Many carry costs which the youngster from a low-income family cannot meet. In a few schools, extra-curricular participation which might bind students to the school is denied those who are not doing well in their classes.

The activities available to him should not be low in prestige as far as the rest of the students are concerned. To meet these requirements, it may be necessary to organize new activities such as hobby clubs, based on the present, socially acceptable interests of a number of potential drop-outs. Settlement houses and other groups working with underprivileged youth may have much to offer schools in this respect. It should also be possible for the potential drop-out to find a place in one of the existing activities if a sympathetic teacher or counselor helps him. The dramatics group, for example, may be a high-prestige organization "run" by youngsters with leadership ability and talent. The potential drop-out may be able, however, to make a contribution, recognized by others, by building or painting sets for a play or taking care of the lighting.

A number of schools have met the problem of costs of extra-curricular activities by financing the program from sources other than charges to the students. In other schools, special funds are available to enable students to take part without stigma in the extra-class life of the school regardless of their ability to pay.[4]

7. **Changes in the marking system.** To lessen the feeling of failure among low achievers, a number of schools now emphasize appraisal of the pupil's performance in relation to his own abilities as well as to the achievement of the rest of the class. Recognition of students who earn high marks may stimulate those who are close to them in achievement; but it many times does not provide incentive to the potential drop-out, whose marks are generally low. Programmed learning in which a student

proceeds at his own pace and corrects his own work, is becoming more popular.

To be effective, a change in the marking system should be accompanied by a change in the school's attitudes toward marks, so that neither teachers nor students think of pupils who make high marks as being altogether good or those with low marks as lacking worthy attributes.

8. Special recognition. Most of the pupils who leave high school before graduation have not received any type of recognition from the school — athletic letters, service pins or certificates, membership in an honor society, election to a student office. Many have given as one of the reasons for dropping out the fact that the social and political activities of their schools were dominated by cliques of pupils to which they did not belong. In schools where this is true, the student body as a whole may need guidance in adopting a sounder set of values for judging others than membership in a closely-knit group.

One reason that ability grouping is effective is that a pupil may excel in a lower ability group whereas he would experience failure if placed in a higher ability group.

9. Work with community agencies. There are many ways in which schools can work with community agencies in trying to solve the drop-out problem. In urban centers a large proportion of potential drop-outs is likely to come from families who already have some connection with social welfare agencies. In such cases, a continuous exchange of information between the school and the agencies involved can be mutually helpful. Either the school or the agency may also be able to locate cases which have not come to the other's attention and which should be referred. Many communities also have psychological or psychiatric clinics to which they can refer those cases whose needs exceed the school's resources.

Another kind of school-community cooperation involves going beyond the school's own internal problems and taking leadership in working with other groups to improve the conditions of those at the lower end of the socio-economic scale. The school can arouse interest by presenting its views of all the complex factors in which the drop-out problem has its roots, to such organizations as service clubs, the League of Women Voters, the Chamber of Commerce, labor unions, and church groups, with an invitation to further study. Each of these organizations will probably perceive the problem in terms of its own special interests — community welfare, preventing juvenile delinquency, slum clearance and housing, advancing business interests, protecting labor's interests, and furthering religious doctrine. But this diversity of viewpoint can be a good thing; it serves to broaden the attack on the problem and brings new resources to its solution.[5]

10. School attendance as a factor in school progress. Studies have shown a close correlation between retardation and dropping from school on the one hand, and irregular attendance on the other.

It is perhaps not too much to say that the holding and drawing power of a school is one of the measurable standards by which its efficiency may be judged. Many things, though, contribute to the creation of a strong holding and drawing power. Some of these are external to the particular school itself; such as the character of the community, its attitude toward education, the nature of the school census, the compulsory attendance laws, and the character of the compulsory attendance service. Others are characteristic of the school as a whole; for example, the organization of the instruction, the different types of school work offered, the emphasis placed on different areas of the instruction, and the types of teachers. Still others lie within the school itself, for which the principal must be held responsible. These would be such things as attention given to the problem, motivation of the school work, and the development of a school spirit.

When a pupil becomes delinquent, the problem begins with his missing an occasional day, then a few more, until he reaches the stage of becoming truant. The basic causes of this may be simple or complex. However, the causes may be divided into the main categories of health, socio-economic status, and family environment. Usually it can be said that behind each case of chronic absenteeism is a social problem of some kind. The homes of the first offenders are visited by attendance counselors. It then becomes necessary to force the pupils into school through the issuance of the "twenty-four legal notices." The attendance counselor then takes over working with families, the social agencies, and the juvenile court.

It is obvious that many students who are socially and economically maladjusted are frequently absent. They feel uncomfortable in a school situation unfamiliar to them. It is vitally important for the teacher to keep constantly in contact with the attendance office and to check immediately regarding absences or tardies and the reasons for them. These should, if possible, be checked the first day of absence, and the teacher should find out when the student returns the reason for his absence. This will keep her alert to many situations which otherwise she might not understand.

There seems to be little danger of placing too much stress on a well-planned, orientation-type program. If students succeed in school, they must become acquainted with the school program and experience the feeling of acceptance by the student body. The counseling staff in each of our high schools has a program of orientation for freshmen which starts when the counselors go to the elementary schools to introduce the high school program to eighth graders and home rooms, in classrooms and assemblies in various forms throughout the year.[6]

11. **The case conference method** (to be dealt with in more detail in the next chapter) *is an effective method of fighting the drop-out problem.*

In summary, then, we find:

1. *The curriculum of the high school needs to offer courses more adapted to the interests and abilities of disadvantaged students as well as courses suited to the needs of accelerated students.*

2. *The high school needs to improve guidance services.*

3. *Pupil cumulative records should provide more information needed for adequate pupil guidance.*

4. *The classroom should communicate to the student how it fulfills his immediate needs.*

5. *Pupils should be grouped carefully according to their abilities.*

6. *Extra-curricular activities should include some which are geared to the interests and abilities of the potential drop-out.*

7. *Appraisal of pupil performance needs to be in relation to his own abilities.*

8. *Special recognition needs to be given to the potential drop-out.*

9. *Schools should correlate their work with community agencies.*

10. *Of vital importance is immediate and continuous checking on school attendance.*

11. *The case conference method may be used to fight the drop-out problem.*

ENDNOTES

1. Penty, Dr. Ruth C., "Reading Ability and High School Drop-Outs," Bureau of Publications, New York, Teachers' College, p. 42, 1956.
2. Caravello, S. J., "The Drop-Out Problem," High School Journal, 41:355–40, 1958.
3. *Ibid.*, 41:336.

4. Allen, Charles M., "Combatting the Drop-Out Problem, Chicago, Science Research Associates, pp. 42–43.
5. *Ibid.,* p. 46.
6. Shepp, D. W., "Can We Salvage the Drop-Outs?" Clearing House, 31:49–54, 1956.

QUESTIONS

1. What is the correlation between lack of reading ability and dropping out of school?
2. What correlation is there between inability to read and delinquency?
3. What are some problems which the drop-out faces?
4. What suggestions could be made to improve secondary education and reduce the drop-out rate?
5. How does irregular attendance play a role in the drop-out situation? Why must a teacher become especially alert to absenteeism and its causes?

Chapter 8

USE OF THE CASE CONFERENCE

The case conference is one media to use in fighting the drop-out problem.

In organizing the case conference, a number of people select several pupils for intensive study; then someone must give time to organizing the conferences. A chairperson and a secretary for each meeting should be chosen, some information collected in advance, and participants invited. To be successful, it is often more effective if organized by a teacher, counselor, or homeroom teacher instead of by someone in a high official position, thus avoiding any subtle administrative pressures.

It is well to have a chairperson who is one skillful in conducting meetings of small groups and familiar with case conference procedures. Since that person's duties are to help the group gain all the facts it needs regarding each pupil and to reach an agreement regarding solutions for problems, the chairperson should not defend proposals of his own but should remain objective. The secretary of the meeting should perform the usual duties of keeping notes regarding the information collected and the action taken and recording these matters for the files of the students.

HOW TO ORGANIZE THE CASE CONFERENCE

The organizer of the conference should take the responsibility of inviting the participants. He/She should set the time of the meeting several days in advance, and at least an hour-and-a-half should be allowed for each of the first few meetings. Those participating should be all the teachers who have the pupil in classes, in extra-curricular activities plus any teachers who have known the student especially well in past years. His counselor and possibly an administrator should be there. If specialists in guidance or psychology are available either in the school or the community, they should also be asked to attend. The school nurse or local social worker also often prove helpful.

Before the conference, information about the case should be collected from any sources that will not be represented at the meeting. School records should be utilized to provide school grades, test results, information about attendance and any participation in extra-curricular activities as well as reports of physical exams. Sources should be consulted regarding any truancy or contact with truant officers or relations with juvenile court personnel. Useful information found in school records or any which can be obtained from other sources should also be included.

The case conference should not be open to all but should be limited to teachers and professionally trained individuals. That way there can be absolute freedom of discussion so that the conference will be productive.

HOW SHOULD THE CASE CONFERENCE BE CONDUCTED?

The chairperson first of all should open the meeting and ask if the pupil in question is a potential drop-out. If he/she is, the group as a whole should consider how that person can be helped to stay in school. Observations from different perspectives should be expressed. That is, the nurse will have input which varies from the input of the teacher, and the counselor or juvenile authority will have even a different perspective.

Those who selected the special case under consideration can then tell the reasons *why* the pupil is regarded as a potential drop-out. Other members of the group may wish to contribute from their backgrounds of knowledge regarding the forces which influence the pupil to stay in school or to leave school. It is important that those in the group be specific regarding their observations of why they feel the pupil is a potential drop-out and not make broad statements of subjective judgments.

Sometimes it will be difficult to gain a reasonably complete picture regarding the subject because of lack of full information regarding home background, the pupil's personal friends, and other factors. The group may decide to further explore these matters before another meeting.

The focus of the group should be on the special things which they as a group can do to keep the person in school. For example, if the major difficulty is a reading disability, perhaps a tutor could be engaged to help the pupil. If, on the other hand, the pupil is inattentive because of health problems, a very different solution would, obviously, be forthcoming as an answer.

When the group has arrived at a decision, or some decisions, regarding what are the basic causes of the pupil's difficulty, there should be definite assignments regarding who will assume the responsibility of acquiring additional information and/or helping to provide a solution.

A future date for reporting back to the group should be decided on, and the group should plan to meet before long for further action.

Sometimes the result of the conference is only an educational process so that a teacher may operate within a more intelligent framework of understanding.

A CASE CONFERENCE MUST BE KEPT CONFIDENTIAL

The information acquired at the case conference should definitely be kept confidential. Professionals involved in such a conference should certainly be aware of this, but it may be well to emphasize the fact.

The case conference is a very effective technique in helping teachers better understand the ones with whom they are working. It also helps develop rapport among faculty involved and is one of the effective ways to approach the problem of students who might be potential drop-outs.

QUESTIONS

1. Who might organize a case conference?
2. What are some pointers which might be helpful to know in organizing the case conference?
3. Who might be included, and what type of input might each have?
4. What follow-up might be planned to help make the conference effective?
5. Summarize some of the advantages of planning a case conference.

Chapter 9

LEARN TO UNDERSTAND
THE STUDENT'S WORLD

It is with great difficulty that the beginning teacher can understand many of the customs and habits of those whose world is so vastly different from hers/his. Nevertheless it is incumbent upon the novice teacher to learn to project to the different background of students at least enough to gain a semblance of understanding regarding where they are coming from.

The children of poverty—especially in our cities, minority children—remain prisoners of a long and brutalizing legacy of racism and economic exile. Repeating generations of unemployment, welfare, dead-end futility, have worked to shatter the family structure, leaving many youngsters without the role focus of fathers, and with mothers so overwhelmed by pressures, they are unable to provide discipline and order in their children's lives. Those families, largely but not all minority, have been trapped in America's urban ghettos and pockets of rural poverty so long, that they have lost real connections to the work ethic . . . lost any hope or vision that they might have transferred to their children to help them escape through schooling. From homes usually barren of books, of any vocabulary of ideas, they enter school already lagging behind and, year after year, fall yet further behind.[1]

Much of the behavior of slum children is emotionally upsetting to middle-class teachers. The most disturbing is that which is radically different from the typical upbringing and experience of the teacher who often grew up in a comfortable, nonslum home. The slum child's behaviors that are most striking are those related to violence, cleanliness, property, sex, and responsibility.[2]

In Joe Clark's remarkable book, LAYING DOWN THE LAW, he, as a new principal at Eastside High School in Paterson, New Jersey, spells out how he was able to transform an inner-city school from one of no discipline and a community riddled with crime into a well-organized, positive educational institution. Part of his success was due to the fact that he had grown up in overcrowded, slum conditions and understood the milieu of the underworld. Before school opened in the fall, he, as the new principal, had the school renovated, graffiti removed, and established a decorum of orderliness. Then before the students and teachers arrived for the fall semester, he mailed to the staff and teaching corps a newly drawn up suspension policy for that year. He brought about order where there had previously been chaos, and his unorthodox methods have made him the subject of controversy both inside and outside the school, though none can doubt his remarkable results, or his popularity with parents and students. His success at Eastside has won him the plaudits of many, including former Secretary of Education William J. Bennett. He is the subject of the major motion picture, "Lean on Me" and has appeared on "Donahue," "Nightline," "60 Minutes," and numerous other television shows.[3]

VIOLENCE

Many children in the slums fight for survival to protect themselves from others, and others also fight to gain status and prestige in the eyes of their peers. Some parents encourage their children to stand up and fight for themselves.[4]

From childhood the middle-class teacher is taught to feel distaste and disgust and even anger when exposed to dirty, messy, filthy, smelly, and sweaty things and people. Many teachers react with just these feelings to slum children.[5]

Relations between administrators and teachers with parents often are approached as though this were still a nation of Ozzies and Harriets. But the new reality is that the father who used to return from a hard day's work faithfully each evening to his homemaking wife and their two well-adjusted children is probably now living alone in a bleak apartment somewhere trying to figure out how to pay for his TV dinners after writing the weekly alimony check. The mother, who remained behind with the children in the prototypical split-level house, has joined a conscious-raising group and works three days a week performing menial tasks in an office, struggling to reactivate and augment job skills that she has not used since she was twenty years old. And the children—yes, the children—are facing awesome tasks of building their educational future on a support system of splinters.[6]

CLEANLINESS

Middle-class homes stress that "Cleanliness is next to Godliness." Children who are underprivileged and have not had access to the same regularity of taking baths, of having swimming pools, and of being cared for are sometimes a shock to the middle-class pedagogue.

Fewer children are living with both biological parents, more children are sharing a home with an adult partner of their mother who is not their father, and more children are being born into homes in which no father resides or ever will reside. In the 1990's, only half the households in the country are expected to contain a married couple. The remaining households will contain only one adult or an unmarried couple living together, and school children will live in many of these homes. It was found that in 1978 more than half of the nation's mothers—whether living with another adult or not—were in the paid labor force, and the proportion will continue to grow. Apparently, the family portrait of the immediate post-World War II era, the never-divorced couple of working father, homebound mother, and their children, is becoming so rare that it may soon be an artifact appropriate for the Smithsonian. Such families are expected to comprise 14 percent of all households in the 1990's.[7]

PRIVATE PROPERTY

The young slum child who does not have a sense of ownership does not feel the sense of property. Ownership and acquisition are often at the bottom of his list of priorities. Many slum children come from large families who use and borrow each others' clothes and possessions regularly whereas the middle-class child from a home where there are one or two children has been taught a very definite sense of property. Then when the child from the slums comes to school and uses or "borrows" property of the other children, he is faced with the fact that he is stealing.

PUNCTUALITY

Middle class families are often very time conscious as opposed to children with Mexican or Latin backgrounds where time takes on an entirely different meaning. It is helpful if a teacher understands the much slower pace of many of the children who have not been raised to be confined to time schedules nor taught to hurry. It is well for a teacher to study the habit patterns of the various ethnic groups. The cumulative records in the school office can be of valuable assistance.

LANGUAGE

Pupils from different ethnic groups have vastly different speech patterns, and it is extremely important for a teacher to constantly evaluate exactly what it is that has been communicated. One must teach within the student's framework, and that may be a real challenge to discover.

RACE

Feelings about race in this country are disquieting to say the least. They can quickly bubble over into a variety of negative and guilty feelings, explosions of hate and acts of violence. These feelings are well known between the white and black races, but feelings also run high between whites and Puerto Ricans, whites and Mexican-Americans, whites and American Indians.[8]

Teachers are also exposed to racial feelings in the community at large.[9]

A clever teacher can sometimes solve conflict problems with seat assignments which help to avoid tensions between some who have these difficulties.

SEXUALITY

Another area of high emotion for middle-class teachers is the expression of sexual feelings. Sexuality is expressed in the classroom in many ways by pupils and teachers—sometimes more openly, other times disguised; sometimes frankly, other times shyly, sometimes comfortably, at other times with anxiety.[10]

In the slum school, sex presents strong emotional problems for middle-class teachers. Slum children often come from subcultures where all feelings are more directly and openly expressed. For these children sexual feelings are directly expressed and in ways usually quite unfamiliar to the teacher ... Even direct physical expression of sexual interest is often expressed in the classroom. Children will relate specific details of the sexual behavior they have observed at home over the weekend. Many teachers, especially the unmarried, are shocked with these intimate reports.[11]

Here the beginning teacher must keep in mind that these children often come from crowded homes where there is little or no privacy, and the adults and children intermingle in a far different way than in middle-class homes where each of the children has a separate bedroom and more space.

SUMMARY

In summary, then, the middle-class teacher who accepts her first assignment may be placed in an entirely different situation, one which is totally foreign to her own background and upbringing. The teacher needs, therefore, to develop a shock-proof constitution and develop a professional and objective attitude, learning as she goes regarding patterns of distinctly different ethnic and cultural groups.

ENDNOTES

1. Frady, Marshall and Dunphy, Joan, *To Save Our Schools, To Save Our Children*, Far Hills, New Horizon, 1985, p. 16.
2. Greenberg, Dr. Herbert M., *Teaching With Feeling*, Macmillan, 1969, p. 73.
3. Clark, Joe with Picard, Joe, *Laying Down the Law*, Washington, DC, Regnery, 1989 (quote from book jacket).
4. Greenberg, *Teaching With Feeling*, p. 73.
5. *Ibid.*, p. 76.
6. Maeroff, Gene I., *Don't Blame the Kids*, New York, McGraw-Hill, 1982, p. 211.
7. *Ibid.*, pp. 211–212.
8. Greenberg, *Teaching With Feeling*, p. 188.
9. *Ibid.*, p. 193.
10. *Ibid.*, p. 178.
11. *Ibid.*, p. 78.

QUESTIONS

1. What were some techniques used by Joe Clark by which a chaotic school situation was transformed into a positive, well-organized educational system?
2. How does the slum child's concept of violence often differ from that of the middle-class pedagogue's?
3. How has the socio-economic situation in homes changed within the last decade?

4. Why are slum children more apt than others sometimes to get into trouble regarding stealing and/or punctuality?
5. Why might a beginning teacher be shocked regarding students' attitudes toward sex?

Chapter 10

UTILIZE COUNSELORS' EXPERTISE

A school counselor can perform many services, and one should not think of counselors only as persons who are concerned with class schedules and filling in applications for students for various reasons.

An alert teacher will, of course, recognize at once when a pupil is emotionally or psychologically disturbed. Not only does the teacher recognize this by noting the student who gets moody or has a temper tantrum or is rude or taunting others, but sometimes students will reveal in essays much of their life history and their problems. However, the teacher's focus needs to be on how that student performs in class, and the joy is that the teacher should not attempt to solve problems for which counselors are professionally trained. One must keep confidential information without sharing it, but one must feel that counselors are invaluable backup helps.

Counselors can help students with personal identity problems, with raising their self-esteem and self-confidence, and with accepting their individual strengths, weaknesses, and differences. Counselors can also help students improve their attitudes toward their family, their school, and/or their community.[1]

CUMULATIVE RECORD FILE

It is very helpful in gaining a better understanding of the pupil with whom one is working if one checks the cumulative record file which is kept in the school office.

As you may know, in it are kept the comments and annotations from teachers who have worked with the pupil all through his/her previous years of schooling. Such records contain referrals to the office when a student has been disciplined, notes regarding his attitudes and/or aptitudes, his health situation, and other facts which can be quite revealing. You, too, will be adding to the case history, and if or when you have an unfortunate experience with a student, it is your protection legally if you have kept a short anecdotal record for the file.

Early in my teaching I had a class of the poorer achievers, many of whom had backgrounds of lack of home education and other problems often correlated with those from a more disadvantaged socio-economic group. Usually those in such groups have language patterns which betray their environment plus attitudes either of apathy or resistance to book learning when they begin the year. Since the school in which I taught divided students into homogeneous groupings, this class was composed mostly of those who ranked low on their reading entrance tests.

In that class at the first of the year was a student who was nattily dressed and wore a suit to school while most of the teenagers in that particular school wore jeans. His hair was slicked down, his manners were impeccable, and he read fluently. Consequently I was certain that he had been misplaced and that the counselor was in error in placing him with the others in that homogeneous group. Hence I made an appointment with the counselor who referred me to the cumulative record file. Was I glad that I had checked! For in bold-faced letters at the top of his report in the file, jumping out at me, were the startling letters "GRAND THEFT"! Needless to say, it made me realize then that counselors many times have knowledge and judgment which is often some to which teachers do not have access.

A teacher needs to be very objective and cautious in the remarks which she has placed in the cumulative record file, for, since 1974, when the Buckley Amendment was passed, a teacher can be vulnerable and find herself/himself in trouble with the law. In that year Congress significantly altered the public's right of access to materials previously considered confidential.[2]

The Family Educational Rights and Privacy Act (also known as the Buckley Amendment) guarantees parents the right to have access to their child's school records. It also prohibits release of the records to outsiders without parental permission, except in case of emergency.[3]

Libel is the legal term for written defamation. The statement being made need not be intentionally derogatory; a careless comment or even one intended to benefit may land the defamer in court.[4]

The Buckley Amendment was the result of the emergent awareness of possibly damaging remarks in students' records. This resulted in an outpouring of concern by educators and parents. They alleged that it was wrong that children should be "name-called" with no possible opportunity for vindication or even the opportunity to discover the libel. Hence, parents can now review "any and all official records, files, and data directly related to their children" and "shall have an opportunity for a hearing to challenge the content of their child's school record." Each school and school system must develop specific programs to meet the requirements of this act, and they must also follow general regulations from the Department of Health, Education, and Welfare and the Right of Privacy Act.[5]

A teacher's freedom to write anything about a student—that whatever is written will be cloaked in confidentiality—then, no longer exists. So, teachers must remember that what they write may be read by parent, student, lawyer, and jury. Teachers, then, must be prepared to prove statements factual and to prove that suggestive comments of a seemingly defamatory nature are true. The law places the burden of proving the truth of statements upon the person who makes them.[6]

Thus, one sees that it behooves the teacher to use good judgment about statements which are put into the cumulative record file for all to peruse.

Student records will continue to be important. Teachers must make a professional decision as to what information is valid and validly relates to an educational objective . . . If you feel that a pupil is a moron with limited potential simply because he doesn't happen to like math, a Marxist because his favorite color is red, or an exhibitionist because he once came from the rest room with his pants unzipped, keep it to yourself. Such statements do not belong on permanent records, and teachers who write them may soon be unemployed or defendants in a defamation suit.[7]

The cumulative record file, on the other hand, can be most helpful to the teacher when she checks on such items as the health record of the pupil or past academic performance, or other factual matters. Discussion with counselors regarding such factual matters also can help give one insight, but it is no doubt wise not to express value judgments.[8]

GUIDELINES REGARDING LIBEL AND SLANDER

1. Limit discussion of and written statements about individual students and fellow educators to statements that you know or reasonably know to be true.
2. Limit discussion of and written statements about individual pupils

and fellow educators to statements that have a valid educational purpose.

3. If you must make possibly damaging and controversial statements you know to be true and which you believe to have an educationally valid purpose, retain the evidence from which you drew your conclusions.

4. Ask yourself if the evidence of truth of a damaging statement would hold up in court. Ask yourself if it is the sort of evidence that a jury of your neighbors would believe. If not, reconsider making your statements.

5. Remember that parents and pupils have expanded rights to examine documents under the Buckley Amendment. Consider that third persons outside the school may see or hear your statements.

6. Never make statements or write reports in the heat of anger. Delay saying potentially dangerous, damaging, or libelous things.

7. Whenever possible, talk directly to persons involved to determine the source of damaging statements and to verify the truth.

8. Before making or writing any statement, ask if it holds another up to contempt, hatred, or ridicule. If so, be especially sure of the truth of the statement and of the educational purpose in repeating it.

9. Never, never expect that statements made in confidence to pupils or in the teachers' lounge will not be repeated.[8]

ENDNOTES

1. Albert, Linda, *Coping With Kids and School*, New York, E. P. Dutton, 1984, p. 135.
2. Strickland, Phillips, and Phillips, *Avoiding Teacher Malpractice*, New York, Hawthorn, 1976, p. 78.
3. Schimmel, David and Fischer, Louis, *Parents, Schools, and the Law*, (2nd Ed.), Natl. Comm. for Citizens in Ed., 1988, p. 168.
4. Strickland, Phillips, and Phillips, *Avoiding Teacher Malpractice*, p. 78.
5. and 6. *Ibid.*, p. 83.
7. *Ibid.*, p. 84.
8. *Ibid.*, p. 85.

QUESTIONS

1. Define libel.
2. Why might it be important to check a pupil's cumulative record?
3. How are some ways counselors can help your teaching?
4. Explain how the Buckley Amendment of 1974 could affect you as a teacher.
5. What guidelines might you keep in mind to protect yourself against any danger of becoming liable?

Chapter 11

UTILIZE SCHOOL AND COMMUNITY RESOURCES

I t is important for a teacher to learn how to tap the resources both of her/his own school and of the community. Different schools, of course, have different available helps, but most schools provide the services of a school nurse, school librarians, a counselor (or counselors), a school psychologist, a custodian, and other helpers. Within the community a social worker who has records regarding some students is also available. These can prove to be valuable assets to any instructor.

THE INDISPENSABLE LIBRARIANS

If you're teaching any academic subject, it's great to have as your best friends the librarians. Especially if you're teaching Social Studies or English, what better than to expose your students to the wisdom of the ages, in the library?

I have found that librarians can be most helpful and that if students have learned the basics of using computers and knowing their way about in the library, then there are resources available there which can keep them busy, interested, and occupied for hours and which never could be had in the classroom.

Another advantage of utilization of the library as a class group is that students like the freedom of being able to leave their classroom occasionally. Many times I would have students just sign in when they arrive at the library and then they are free to move about where they need to so long as they sign out when they leave. They enjoy the liberty of pursuing their assignments on their own initiative.

School librarians have a knack of matching books to the students, and they like to learn the student's interests and reading levels.[1]

Librarians can help by suggesting articles or stories for those with reading problems, articles that will capture interest without being too difficult to read. Often they can steer the student to magazines, audio tapes, and/or records which will entice them to read.

He or she often knows the school curriculum and has an informal relationship with the student, and many times librarians pride themselves on getting to know the students personally and in finding for them books of special appeal.

Librarians can also suggest special book review sessions and other resources which can motivate classes for further study.

THE SCHOOL NURSE

Sometimes the school nurse is only an aide or a para-professional with little training, depending upon the particular school situation. Other schools employ nurses who have earned both nursing and teaching degrees. Obviously, it goes without saying that the more training and expertise which a school nurse has obtained, the more services she can render both to the child, the parent, and the teacher.[2]

The school nurse can treat minor cuts and bruises but should refer serious accidents or illnesses to the proper medical personnel.

Be alert to your utilization of the advice and services of the school nurse.

The *first day* in which I taught in one school (that most hectic of days when one is trying to get standards set, pupils assigned to seats, and a precedent set for the entire school year) a little girl came up to my desk and said she didn't feel well. I sent her to her seat and told her to put her head down on her desk, but I did not send her to the nurse as I should have. The next day I found that she had had a streak up her arm and that she had blood poisoning. Fortunately, she got immediate care. Not only should I have sent her summarily to the nurse on that first day for her own health and safety but for my own also in avoiding any possible liability suit.

In most schools it is now against the law for a teacher to give a student any medication (even an aspirin), but the teacher should be cognizant of the fact that the student who has any kind of ailment should be sent immediately to the nurse. Certainly there are times when students might feign illness to get out of class, but then the nurse can evaluate that situation. It is important, however, for the teacher to be sure to have the student give an accountability either in having a slip signed by the nurse as to the time when he/she was in the nurse's office or a report in some fashion; otherwise, students have been known to have used going to the nurse as an excuse to leave the school premises.

Also to be noted is for a teacher to keep close contact with the nurse in case a pupil has had some serious illness and then returns to school.

Student academic achievement certainly often can be closely related to a student's health situation.

SCHOOL COUNSELORS

Another chapter deals with the fact that the school counselors are an integral part of the teacher's becoming effective in her profession.

THE SCHOOL PSYCHOLOGIST

School psychologists are especially trained in working with individuals in both individual therapy and family therapy. Through tests which have been skillfully developed, they evaluate and determine the needs and programs for children or young people who are experiencing difficulties in school.[3]

THE SOCIAL WORKER

It is well for the teacher to be at least knowledgeable regarding agencies in the state government which work with children and young people. Sometimes cumulative records reveal whether a pupil is getting help through state agencies. The Department of Economic Security works with those of different ages, but, depending upon the age of the child, young person, or adult who is in your class, a social worker may be working with the individual or families, and a teacher should at least know that there are such agencies.

In the Department of Economic Security in the state government there are the following agencies: Child Support Enforcement Administration, Child Protective Services, and Family Assistance. Those are but some of the agencies which in the state government work with some of your students.

Many of the students may already be connected with family social workers, and it may be helpful, possibly through the school counselor, to make contact with those who already have the case histories of the ones with whom you are working and to coordinate efforts. The teacher can much better understand the one with whom she/he is working if one knows the existing case histories.

THE CUSTODIAN

Many times custodians are carefully screened by the Administration, and if a teacher establishes a certain rapport with the custodian, many times the "Grapevine," to which the custodian is often connected, can give one information and helps regarding the total school situation. For example, a custodian may have heard the plans of a certain school gang as to their after-school activities, and sometimes trouble can be averted.

Never under-estimate the importance of the non-certificated staff— those of the custodial or cafeteria group. They are an essential, vitally important segment of the total school picture.

PARENTS

Of course at the elementary and middle school levels particularly, getting to know and establish positive relationships with the parents is the key to how to educate their children so far as getting to know the pupil's background is concerned. Many times the student whose parents are involved in the Parent-Teachers Association, or, at the elementary level, in assisting in many ways, is the student about whom one does not have to be unduly concerned.

In summary, then, keep in mind that a teacher's load can be greatly lightened if one maintains contact with the school nurse, the parents, the school counselor, the librarian, the school psychologist, possibly the social worker, and the non-certificated staff. Obviously, satisfactory relationships with the Administration and the Board are at the top of the list. In other words, teaching consists of a total team effort which undergirds the focus upon helping and educating the "whole child."

ENDNOTES

1. Albert, *Coping With Kids and School,* New York, Dutton, 1984, p. 133.
2. *Ibid.,* p. 137.
3. *Ibid.,* p. 138.

QUESTIONS

1. How important is it to utilize the services of the school nurse?
2. In what ways can the school librarians lighten your load?
3. How can getting to know a child's parents prove helpful?
4. The knowledge of what other personnel in the pupil's life can prove informative and helpful?
5. What role can the non-certificated employees, such as the custodian and the cafeteria workers, play?

Chapter 12

VARIETY IS THE SPICE

Children of the 1990's are oriented to a world of visual media—TV, maps, posters, charts, plus audio media of radio and sound media. All can be used to bring vitality to the message of the curricula.

Much visual media can be made by a creative teacher who is not an artist but who can learn easily techniques of creating such.

One especially useful and helpful book—*Handbook for Preparing Visual Media* by Ed Minor (Professor of Communications, Sacramento State University, Sacramento, California), has proven to be particularly helpful.

This book contains the following chapters:

1—**VISUAL MEDIA PREPARATION GUIDELINES**—This is concerned with ideas, designing, lettering, and coloring.[1]

2—**VISUAL IMAGING**—This chapter suggests specific aids for drawing tools, cutting tools, photosketch imaging, and the like.[2]

3—**SPECIAL EFFECTS FOR IMAGES**—Coloring images have to do with color with pencils, pens, liquid colors, spray-can colors, transparent color sheets, pattern and shading films.[3]

4—**LETTERING MADE SIMPLE**—This chapter gives special helps for many various types of lettering and how to make such—stencil lettering, vinyl plastic letters, rubber stamp printing, spray-on lettering, bulletin typewriter lettering, and many other kinds of lettering.[4]

5—**MOUNTING AND LAMINATING IMAGES**—Do you need help with mounting? Here is your answer. A chapter on mounting aids, bulletin board mounting, double-coated adhesive mounting, dry backing cloth mounting, heat and cold laminating acetate images.[5]

6—**SIMPLE DISPLAY MAKING**—Here is a chapter which deals with simple display making for educational displays and exhibits and with trend ideas for making better bulletin boards and displays.[6]

7—**TRANSPARENCIES**—Guidelines for making transparencies are given. The advantage of transparencies is that an instructor can work out his own lesson ideas and materials and develop his own specific transparencies.[7]

59

There is help in Chapter 7 in making transparencies for study and display. The author deals with cold laminating acetate image transfer transparencies, rubber cement image transfer transparencies, electronic stencil transparencies, and types of slides such as direct image, thermocopy, xerograph, and slide guide sheets.

Other similar books of this type can provide specific helps.

If the instructor is fortunate enough to have an Audio-Visual Department in which experts are employed to make the above media, certainly a teacher could very well follow through with the above suggestions and explain to the experts the specific type of media which would prove most useful in one's particular situation.

If, on the other hand, the instructor is not so fortunate as to have an adequate Audio-Visual person or department, then one could find helpful and valuable suggestions and learn techniques suggested.

Discover who are your art students and utilize their talents. This will give the students an especially useful motivation for their studies, and you may be surprised what valuable talent is currently within your own classrooms.

It may be also that parents could provide much practical help and/or counsel by utilizing their artistic skills. Besides being of special help to the teacher, such utilization of parent talent makes for positive and compatible public relations.

APPEAL TO ALL OF THE STUDENTS' FACULTIES

A revolution in our understanding of learning itself is well under way. It has to do with the nature of intelligence: there is a lot more to it than how well we deal with mathematics and language, the skills tested by the SATs and other standardized exams. According to Harvard psychologist Howard Gardner, we all have at least seven different kinds of intelligence in varying degrees. In addition to the linguistic and logical-mathematical talents measured by most standardized tests, there are special intelligences that deal with spatial awareness, bodily-kinesthetic functions, music, inter-personal relationships, and self-understanding. Students learn a lot faster when their courses are designed to appeal to all of these faculties rather than in lecture-and-workbook classes.[8]

ENDNOTES

1–7. Minor, Ed, *Handbook for Preparing Visual Media,* (2nd Ed.), New York, McGraw-Hill, 1978, pp. 9, 37, 41, 53, 95, 117, 125.
8. Cetron, Marvin and Gayle, Margaret, *Educational Renaissance,* New York, St. Martin's, 1991, p. 120.

QUESTIONS

1. What are some visual media which can be utilized?
2. What types of lettering are suggested?
3. How, other than through the Audio-Visual Department, can one get art work done? Why might that be useful?

Chapter 13

SUPPORT GROUPS FOR THE NEW TEACHER

Why is the first year such a nightmare for the beginning teacher? The teacher had approached the situation so idealistically and then all her dreams seem shattered. There are several reasons for disillusionment, but if the beginning teacher can be patient and survive that first year, each subsequent year will no doubt improve.

In the first place, the new teacher is almost inevitably given the most difficult assignment in the system. It is only logical that the longer the tenure of one within the system, the more desirable assignment he/she asks for and usually will receive. Each year a teacher strives for promotion; hence the poorest and most difficult jobs are, ironically, foisted off on the most inexperienced teachers.

In one school in which I taught when I was a new teacher in a system in California, it was during the time when if Los Angeles had built one new school each week, the Administration still would not have been able to keep ahead of the influx of population into the state.

I, as a beginning teacher in California, was assigned, because I was the newest teacher hired, to handle the overflow from other classes. Such was to be the composition of my class. Each teacher was to send two pupils from each of her/his classes. If you were asked to do that, which two pupils would you send? Obviously, I was given the two worst discipline cases from each of the several classes, and the entire faculty seemed to be watching to know the outcome. Fortunately, I was able to survive, and why? Because I had some undergirding support.

What are some of the supportive influences which can make the difference in whether or not that new person can endure the rigors of that first horrible year?

1—OTHER TEACHERS CAN PROVIDE HELP

Before the days of Merit Pay, it was customary for the more seasoned teachers in the profession, in a friendly way, to befriend the newer teachers with practical help regarding the school facilities, with materials they had found especially effective, and with counsel regarding daily problem situations. Because one of those more experienced teachers acted as something of a Big Sister in one of my new situations, we developed a lifelong friendship.

2—HELP FROM A MASTER TEACHER OR SUPERVISOR

If a master teacher is willing to share her own real, initial teaching experience with the beginner, this can reduce some of the heightened emotion and tension of the new teacher. The new teacher can feel fewer fears about his own "normality."[1]

3—THE RIGHT KIND OF TEACHER PREPARATION

So many teachers complain that their education classes in college were not of enough real practical help. If one finds this to be true, there are many practical books regarding teaching which can be found in the local library which can prove helpful in offering real and pertinent tips regarding techniques of teaching.

4—THE COFFEE BREAK

Coffee break time can be either very devastating, or it can prove important. From companionship with one's peers on the faculty, much can be learned regarding current attitudes of teachers and pupils alike, and many tips regarding the politics of the school situation.

There are, within the school geography, certain places—the staff room, the teachers' lounge, a table or alcove in the cafeteria set aside for faculty—where the faculty meets informally. It is here—most often in the staff room—that cliques are formed, and alignments made and broken. It is here that gossip and rumor are shared, along with the exchange of laughter and indignation, and the discussion of possible methods of infringement on, or circumnavigation of, the regulations. It is here that the staff discusses the principal, as well as the children and their parents. A clever and power-hungry teacher finds the staff room fertile ground for planting seeds of dissension. Here, too, friendships are made and personal problems come to light.[2]

To study a staff room as people come in and out is a fascinating way to see how power emerges in a group, where the morale, the tone, of the school comes from, and how the leader is and remains the delineating factor.[3]

5—CHILDREN, THEMSELVES, CAN PROVIDE SUPPORT

Remarks offered spontaneously in the midst of apparent chaos are particularly heartwarming.

"You're great. I will miss you," or "We missed you when you were sick." Remarks like this, notes from the students, or gifts offered by them are all evidence of positive, successful response.[4]

6—PARENTS ALSO CAN BE SUPPORTIVE.

Parents also can offer real and spontaneous praise, which can assist a teacher in gaining a more balanced perspective about her success and her accomplishment.[5]

7—PRINCIPALS CAN ASSIST

Principals and supervisors can assist greatly when they are able to relieve a new teacher of a particularly troublesome child. Sending the pupil down to the office can be of considerable help to a new teacher when she "is at the end of her rope" and nothing seems to work.[6]

This should be done early in the year, however, or even the first day or two. Although many times the new teacher tries to be patient, it is far better not to lose the initial control because of waiting too long to enlist the help of a principal or supervisor.

In a National Education Association study of why teachers leave teaching, it was found that interpersonal conflicts—with fellow teachers and the Administration—and poor resources were chosen relatively infrequently at all levels as reasons for leaving teaching. Even problems with students ranked low. It was personal frustration and dissatisfaction in the teaching situation that appeared to bother most teachers. If one goes into teaching with expectations of being able to teach and be of service and then is frustrated in realizing these expectations, dissatisfaction sets in and quitting becomes an alternative.[7]

It is interesting that though money was not a major reason teachers gave for entering teaching, it ranked second as a reason for leaving. We might speculate that, anticipating rewards intrinsic to the work, teaching began with a willingness to forego high salaries. However, when confronted with the frustrations of those expectations, the fact that they sometimes are paid less than the bus drivers who bring their students to school may become a considerable source of dissatisfaction as well.[8]

Advice to the beginning teacher, then, would be to utilize the supportiveness of other teachers, of the supervisor, of book resources, of the coffee break discussions, of positive children and parents, and of the principal. Developing these positive associations can provide real compensation for the more difficult moments.

ENDNOTES

1. Greenberg, Dr. Herbert M., *Teaching With Feeling*, New York, Macmillan, 1969, p. 108.
2. Newman, Dr. Ruth G., *Groups in Schools*, New York, Simon and Schuster, 1974, p. 144.
3. *Ibid.*, p. 145.
4 and 5. Greenberg, *Teaching With Feeling*, p. 114.
6. *Ibid.*, pp. 112–113.
7. Goodlad, John I., *A Place Called School*, New York, McGraw-Hill, 1983, p. 172.
8. *Ibid.*, p. 172.

QUESTIONS

1. How can other teachers, specifically, provide help?
2. If one feels that one's practice teaching did not entirely prepare her/him for the "real world" of the classroom, where else might he/she find help?
3. Comment on how the "coffee break" can be a positive or negative influence in a school.
4. List other sources where supportiveness might be found.

Chapter 14

AVOID BEING SUED

Because a teacher is considered *in loco parentis* (in place of the parent), a teacher must be alert at all times to the possibilities of problems, particularly in this day and age of parent lawsuits against teachers. This does not mean for a teacher not to operate with confidence and poise but only to be aware of possible trouble situations. Many districts have liability insurance to protect the instructor in the event that a parent should bring a law suit. Hence it is well to know the background of the school law suits and the danger involved if one is not cognizant of the fact that the pupils have certain rights and that there are certain standards of professional conduct for the teachers. In case one is not knowledgeable regarding students' rights and teachers' responsibilities, trouble could develop.

PROFESSIONAL CONDUCT OF TEACHERS— KNOW YOUR RIGHTS AS A TEACHER

So, what is considered "professional conduct"? It might be well to consider what courts of law have ruled as "professional conduct" and actions which they have ruled as not within the jurisdiction of the rights of the instructor. Listed here are a few court cases and the result of the court's rulings.

COURT CASE

L.A. VALLEY v. STANFORD (1947)

A suit against the physical education teacher. Injuries were received by a pupil participating in a physical activity—boxing with another pupil.

The defendant won the suit because the court felt it the duty of a teacher to exercise care to prevent injuries.[1]

BAKER v. OWEN (1975)

Russell Carl (a sixth-grader) was paddled on December 6, 1973

66

even though Mrs. Baker had previously requested that he not be corporally punished because she opposed in principle corporal punishment.

The court determined that the punishment of Russell Carl Baker did not violate the Fourteenth Amendment rights and that his punishment was not cruel and unusual within the meaning of the Eighth Amendment.[2]

LINDROS v. GOVERNING BOARD OF TORRANCE UNIFIED SCHOOL DISTRICT (1973)

At the end of the 1969–70 academic year, the Governing Board of the Torrance Unified School District terminated petitioner Stanley Lindros, a probationary teacher, because he read a theme to his English class which contained controversial language. No disruption of classroom activities followed petitioner's reading of the selection. No complaint arose from the students and none arose from the parents of the students.

The court concluded that the Board had failed to show that the inclusion of opprobrious language currently used in many subcultures, in a single composition, presented solely for teaching purposes, was a legal cause for severance of a teacher from his employment.[3]

Other cases in which the Supreme Court vacated criminal convictions for offensive speech and remanded in light of a case of Cohen v. California (1971) were Rosenfeld v. New Jersey (1972), Brown v. Oklahoma and Lewis v. City of New Orleans (1972). These cases upheld the use of divergent and distasteful patterns of speech in sections of our multifarious society and an increasing immunity from criminal sanction for such expressions. These rulings do not by any means legitimize the general use of offensive language in the classroom, but they do explain the background and reasons for the use of such words in the teaching of literary works depicting realistically the coarse and strident forms of communication that so often attend public dialogue today.

COURT CASE	**HOW DEALT WITH?**
TINKER v. DES MOINES INDEPENDENT COMMUNITY SCHOOL DISTRICT (1969)	John F. Tinker (15 yr. old) and Christopher Eckhardt (16 yr. old) wore armbands to high school to publicize their objection to the war in Vietnam.

The principals of the Des Moines schools had become aware of the plan to wear the black armbands, and on December 14, 1965, the principals met and adopted a policy that any student wearing an armband to school would be asked to remove it, and if he refused he would be suspended until he returned without the armband.

On December 16th and 17th some of the students wore the armbands and were suspended from school until they would come back without the armbands.

There was no indication that the work of the schools or any class was disrupted. Some remarks were made outside the classroom but there were no threats or acts of violence on school premises.

The District Court recognized that the wearing of an armband for the purpose of expressing certain views is the type of symbolic act that is within the Free Speech Clause of the First Amendment.[4]

ENDNOTES

1. Strickland, Phillips, and Phillips, *Avoiding Teacher Malpractice,* New York, Hawthorn, 1976, p. 145
2. *Ibid.,* pp. 150–153.

3. *Ibid.*, pp. 156–159.
4. *Ibid.*, pp. 153–156.

QUESTIONS

1. Is a teacher responsible for preventing injuries? Cite a case which pertains to this problem.
2. How much latitude does a teacher have in reading an article which might include some opprobrious language. Cite a case in which the teacher was terminated because of his reading such.
3. What was decided by the court regarding wearing an armband for the purpose of expressing certain views?
4. What other cases, perhaps more recent, can you find in your research which may have set precedents which could affect your teaching?

Chapter 15

KNOW THE STUDENTS' RIGHTS

Amendments I, IV, V, VIII, and XIV of the Constitution give the Constitutional provisions safeguarding the individual rights and liberties of individuals. It is well for a teacher to be cognizant of the rights which the students enjoy.

The state's right to provide for schooling is based on the Tenth Amendment. When there is disagreement concerning the limits of school authority and the limits of student freedoms, the issues frequently involve freedom of speech, due process rights, or the student's right to privacy.[1]

The student's right to freedom of expression has certain limits. School authorities need to show (1) that the limitation is needed to ensure that the normal operation of the school will not be disrupted or (2) that the exercise of the freedom is harmful to the well-being and health of the other students. The limitation cannot be arbitrary and without a legitimate state purpose. Courts have not encouraged the use of prior restraint by school authorities. It must be accompanied by procedures that are clear, reasonable, and related to the safety, health, and welfare of the students.[2]

Because of the increase in violent crime and drug use in our society, school authorities, in combatting these problems, have utilized search procedures that have been questioned by some as abridging a student's privacy rights.[3]

Law enforcement officials must present to an officer of the court information that indicates probable cause for a search. Then when the court official is satisfied, he can then issue a search warrant giving authority for a search. Courts have not as a rule required such probable cause standards from school officials. The courts recognize that school officials have the safety and well-being of students as their priority of responsibility and have approved of reasonable cause as justification for a search. Reasonable cause is a lower standard than what is required of the law enforcement officials. The school official does not need a warrant. He needs only to have reasonable cause to believe that the student is in possession of something illegal or harmful.[4]

The Fourth Amendment provides the citizen protection against unreasonable searches. On certain occasions school authorities, when they were carrying out their responsibilities, have utilized student searches. Because in recent years school authorities have had to contend with serious problems such as bomb threats, the possession of dangerous weapons by students, and the use and sale of illegal drugs and alcohol, school officials have on occasion searched students as well as the students' lockers and their cars. Was this an infringement of the privacy rights of students in these cases? Let us examine what the courts say regarding such searches.[5]

The following are some selected court cases and the findings regarding student rights and school relationships. A teacher might want to further explore these cases and read them in detail.

CASE	FINDING
Burnside v. Byars (1966)	Symbolic speech approved.
Blackwell v. Issaquena County Board of Education	Wearing of buttons (symbolic speech) disapproved for creating school disturbance.
Tinker v. Des Moines Independent School District (1969)	Wearing of black armbands as protest is protected speech and did not promote disruptive conduct.
Bethel School Dist. No. 403 v. Fraser (1986)	Lewd and indecent speech by a student during a school assembly is not protected speech.
Gambino v. Fairfax County School Board (1977)	School newspaper included as a part of First Amendment protection.
Trachtman v. Anker (1977)	Court upholds school authorities in preventing sex questionnaire from being distributed to students.
Williams v. Spencer (1980)	Court upholds school authorities' ban on distribution of underground newspaper on school grounds.
Goss v. Lopez (1975)	Required due process for students suspended from school.
Bellmir v. Lund (1977)	Strip search for missing money unreasonable.

Doe v. Renfro (1981)	Nude search of student on the basis of dog alert is unreasonable and a violation of student's rights.
New Jersey v. T.I.O. (1985)	Reasonable cause search upheld with findings usable as evidence in juvenile delinquency proceedings.
Baker v. Owen (1975)	Court upholds corporal punishment of student and outlines safeguard procedures
Ingraham v. Wright (1977)	Ban on cruel and unusual punishment does not apply to corporal punishment
Hazelwood School District v. Kuhlmeier (1988)	Prior restraint and censorship by school authorities affirmed.[6]

During recent years, due process has become one of the most important constitutional rights of parents and students. As exclusion from schools, whether by suspension, expulsion, or some other action, became a widely used form of discipline, parents and students challenged some school procedures, leading to a ruling by the United States Supreme Court that a minimum of due process is required—even in cases involving short-term suspensions. This, the Court said, is not an unreasonable burden for schools, since only such rudimentary elements of fairness as informal notice and hearing are required, and this requirement is met if the student is told orally or in writing what his alleged wrongdoing was and what the evidence is against him, and if he is given a chance to tell his side of the story.[7]

If a long-term suspension is the punishment, the courts require more complete procedures. In such situations, parents may insist on a notice and a hearing, and the right to be represented by a lawyer, to cross-examine witnesses and to be given a record of the proceedings. Parents and students also have the right to appeal—usually to higher school authorities and to the school board.[8]

ENDNOTES

1, 2, 3. Walker, Kozma, and Green, *American Education,* San Francisco, West, 1989, p. 276.

4 and 5. *Ibid.,* pp. 269–270.

6. *Ibid.,* p. 277.

7. Schimmel, David and Fischer, Louis, *Parents, Schools, and the Law,* (2nd Printing), Columbia, Natl. Comm. for Citizens in Ed., 1988, p. 32.

8. *Ibid.,* p. 32.

QUESTIONS

1. What specific protection regarding the student's right to freedom of expression has been outlined by the courts? What is it necessary for the school authorities to show?
2. What protection does the student have regarding searches?
3. Are there other protections which the courts have stated students should have?

Chapter 16

KNOW THE PARENTS' RIGHTS

To some of those in control in the schools, parent involvement is anathema. Interestingly enough, it is the parents and other tax-payers who are the ones who finance the schools! It is also the parents themselves who entrust their prize possessions, their children, to the schools. What happens in the schools, as we know, has the greatest impact other than the home, in shaping the children's lives. Nevertheless, many teachers and administrators believe that parents have no right to influence in any way what happens in their children's schooling.[1]

Often daytime meetings are scheduled with little regard for the schedules of working mothers and fathers. Oftentimes schools do not involve parents in curriculum development or in selecting textbooks. Often when organizations are comprised of low-income parents, the schools listen to those who have the power.[2]

Parents do have certain rights legally, however, and there are some rights which they do not enjoy. Let us examine, then, some of the rights which they do and do not have.

PARENTS *DO* HAVE THE RIGHT

TO see the budget and other documents the school administrators prepare for the board.[3]

TO choose to send their children to religious schools.[4]

TO ask to have their children excused from the daily flag salute and Pledge of Allegiance.[5]

TO challenge discriminatory disciplinary practices.[6]

TO challenge discriminatory testing and placement of students.[7]

TO file a written complaint if they believe that local school policies discriminate against blacks, Hispanics, or other minorities.[8]

TO participate in the development of school policy.[9]

TO inspect certain federally funded curricular materials.[10]

TO file complaints under the law.[11]

TO attend and speak up in school board meetings.[12]

PARENTS DO *NOT* HAVE THE RIGHT

TO control school policy and curriculum.[13]

TO require schools to remove books that offend their religious beliefs.[14]

TO enroll their children in a district where they work or own property but do not reside.[15]

TO educate their children at home.[16]

ENDNOTES

1. Maeroff, Gene I., *Don't Blame the Kids,* New York, McGraw-Hill, 1982, p. 208.
2. *Ibid.,* p. 209.
3. Schimmel and Fischer, *Parents, Schools, and the Law,* pp. 223, 54, 56, 81, 82, 83, 135, 141, 142, 222, 134, 137, 162, 163 (14 sentences stating parents' rights).

QUESTIONS

1. List some of the legal rights of parents in relation to the school.
2. List some rights parents do *not* have, legally, in relation to the school situation.

Chapter 17

UTILIZE PARENTS' TALENTS

Many parents take the schools for granted. The reputation of school districts in the United States often has ridiculously little to do with the content of the curriculum or the quality of the teaching. Usually a desirable school system is considered one in a locale in which the families are on the higher end of the socio-economic scale.[1]

FREE SCHOOL MOVEMENT

The concept of greater parent participation and involvement has natural appeal. The so-called Free School Movement, flourishing in the United States during the 1960's, saw small groups of seemingly like-minded parents setting up and sometimes teaching in their own schools. There is, however, a considerable degree of unrealistic romanticism about parents taking over schooling. The founders of free schools frequently found themselves in apparently irreconcilable ideological disputes. As new schools appeared, others, with a life history of just a few years or only a few months, closed.[2]

Having the parents take over completely is different, however, from having parent involvement and utilizing the talents and aid of parents.

TRAINING PARENTS IN LOW SOCIOECONOMIC AREAS

Training parents to be involved and to assist can be a great boon to teachers. Whether one is placed in a higher socioeconomic milieu or in a lower one, parents can be most helpful.

An urban elementary-school teacher said that the single most important factor enabling her to do her best teaching was "wonderful parent cooperation and support. I feel that's very necessary when you are teaching. The children and the families work together with teachers." A high-school mathematics teacher argues, if "children are not learning, it is because adults don't care. That's the bottom line. I have good classes where parents care, and those children do learn."[3]

Another urban elementary-school teacher who called parental involvement "that missing piece to the puzzle" contended that reading scores would not rise until "parents are not only involved in the school, but in the school work of their children." A middle-school teacher who characterized parental involvement in his school as "nonexistent" said that with "very little feedback at all from parents, we're waging war by ourselves." It was clear that many teachers have felt the need to work closely with, and be supported by, parents. As one said, "Kids need that backup from parents. The teachers need that backup from parents."[4]

In California in a Quality Education Project, nearly 200,000 parents and teachers in the state's lowest socioeconomic areas have been trained in how to help their children learn. A strong working relationship has been formed with the business community, higher education, and law enforcement, and hundreds of partnership programs have been initiated.[5]

If parents make sure that their children do their homework, stay on top of their children's performance, and read to their children, student attitudes and performance will soar dramatically. Effective parent-involvement programs have been developed at very low costs per pupil.

THE 1990 FAIRFAX COUNTY PUBLIC SCHOOLS SURVEY

Early in 1990, Forecasting International conducted a public-opinion survey for the Fairfax County VA school system. The purpose was to learn how strongly Fairfax residents support their schools, how good a job they believe local schools are doing, and where they believe changes are still needed. They discovered a community where learning was sure to prosper. In a time when schools across the United States are struggling with low attendance, poor academic performance, and other problems, they found that Fairfax County schools work, and area residents know it. There is no sign that people are growing complacent in their success or are tiring of reform after years of sometimes contentious change.[6]

If parental support is one key to school success, education in Fairfax County has a lot going for it. One parent in four said he or she felt "very involved" with his or her children's schooling, and nearly three-fourths gave themselves at least a 7 or 8 on a ten-point scale of involvement. This commitment, interestingly enough, was at its highest among minority populations that in other communities often seem cut off from their schools. 43 percent of Hispanic parents said they felt themselves to be very involved with their children's education, far more than in the overall population. The reason may be that because they have felt themselves handicapped by an inadequate education, they pay close attention to their children's progress, but also the district's human-relations committee deserves credit for actively recruiting minority parents to the cause of schooling.[7]

Fairfax County residents, on the whole, rated their public schools very highly. 84 percent of those interviewed considered the quality of the schools to be "excellent" or "good," up from 74 percent sixteen years previously. Seventy-seven percent said the schools did a "good job of preparing students for college." This is well above the national average. One-third of respondents on the survey cited the quality of teachers as the Fairfax County Public Schools' greatest strength.[8]

SOME MODEL PROGRAMS

A perfect example of a successful program made possible by a small initial investment is Project 2000, in the Kern Union High School District in Bakersfield, California. The Ford Motor Company and several other corporations are putting up the initial capital, $400 per student (approximately 10 percent of the state's annual per-pupil expenditure) for 100 students each at four high schools.

The project concentrates on the average child, encouraging that student to take more and harder academic courses and go to college. Students and parents must commit themselves to the project. A team of four teachers (English, science, math, and history) at each school plans the curriculum and organizational changes, with the principal's participation, and stays together during the school year with the 100 students. Teachers have common preparation periods. Each school receives a classroom of Macintosh computers, and the program stresses word processing and writing for freshmen. Students are provided role models and heavy counseling support. Substantial funds are provided for staff development, and teachers tackle the problems of how to make complicated subjects accessible to the average student.[9]

Similar projects, such as AVID in San Diego, have doubled or tripled the college-going rates of minority youth and completely transformed their schools' atmosphere by changing the attitude of many previously apathetic students. The same strategy has worked for potential dropouts in the California Partnership Academies program, which has enjoyed substantial success in increasing graduation rates and community college attendance.[10]

Parents and individual students must be involved in the process of designing schools for the future and understand the implications and importance of a commitment to bettering our educational system.[11]

If the United States is to survive as an economic leader, parents—and everyone—must accept responsibility for performance of their local school systems. They must offer themselves as part-time teachers and teaching assistants, and they must work with local political leaders to raise school budgets, and with school administrators to see that money is used to promote effective classes in the core subjects. Above all, they must make certain that their own children understand the importance of a good education and have support.[12]

ENDNOTES

1. Maeroff, Gene I., *Don't Blame the Kids,* New York, McGraw-Hill, 1982, p. 210.
2. Goodlad, John I., *A Place Called School,* New York, McGraw-Hill, 1983, p. 272.
3. Johnson, Susan Moore, *Teachers At Work,* New York, Basic Books, 1990, p. 89.
4. *Ibid.,* p. 89.
5. Cetron, Marvin and Gayle, Margaret, *Educational Renaissance,* New York, 1991, p. 164.
6. *Ibid.,* p. 144.
7 and 8. *Ibid., p. 144.*
9. *Educational Renaissance,* p. 140.
10. *Ibid.,* pp. 169–170.
11. *Ibid.,* p. 41.
12. *op. cit.,* pp. 17–18.

QUESTIONS

1. What did the Quality Education project in California attempt to accomplish?
2. What did the Fairfax County survey reveal regarding what made their schools so successful?
3. Explain the functioning of Project 2000 which was initiated in Kern County Union High School District in Bakersfield, California.

Chapter 18

MAKING TIME YOUR FRIEND—
NOT YOUR ENEMY!

ROGER W. AXFORD, PH.D.

Every one of us has twenty-four hours in the day! Even teachers. How you spend your time will show your professional dedication. There are many requests for your time—from students, administrators, parents, colleagues, lesson plans, advising, coaching—and you must determine your priorities. Only you can control your time.

What are some of the key pointers for time management?

1. BUDGET YOUR TIME.

A good use of the desk calendar will make time your friend. Keeping appointments is a key sign of a real professional. Not over-scheduling will keep you from stress and keep you calm and in control. You are not much use with a nervous breakdown!

2. PRIORITIZE.

Know what is important! If a student wants to see you, that is a high priority. But, if he or she has emotional problems, know when to send him or her to the counselor. You cannot be all things to all people. Your health and mental health come first, students second, their parents third, administration fourth, colleagues fifth. We can't do everything, and the sign of an amateur is to think that he can. By checking your calendar the day before, one can tell if time has been wasted. Your value system will be revealed in your priorities. Good teachers put their priorities in order early in the year. How can we expect our students to be organized if we are not good models for them in time management?

This chapter was written by Doctor Roger W. Axford, President, Recareering Institute, Tempe, Arizona. He is also Professor Emeritus, Adult Education, Arizona State University and authored two previous titles: *Adult Education (Open Door To Lifelong Learning)* and *Successful Recareering: How to Shift Gears Before You are Over the Hill!*

3. LIST JOBS TO BE DONE.

There is satisfaction in checking off a job completed. Making a list of tasks is a good way to determine what next needs to be done. *How to Manage Your Time and Life* by Alan Lakein is a useful tool for those overstressed by too many projects or commitments. Making a list of what is to be done and how long it will take to do it will help you get control of your teaching. Lesson plans are vital, and they take careful thought and time. Ask, How much time for duplicating? For media? For preparation? How much time for questions and answers? Considering these things is all part of being an effective teacher. After planning to have more than enough teaching material, then knowing what to omit is vital! Doctor Enid Miller, former speech instructor at Nebraska Wesleyan University, used to remind her students, "The making of a good speech is a full wastebasket." Eliminate the irrelevant! Emphasize the high points. Check off the completed tasks and you will have the feeling of satisfaction. You can become your own time manager. Make it fun!

4. PROCRASTINATION IS OUR WORST ENEMY!

Most of us are time wasters. We tend not to do today what we can do tomorrow. Discipline is the key to time management. The people who get things done have a tendency to "do it now!" Writing postcards to friends and colleagues can be a great hobby. One can do this while one is waiting for administrators, waiting for a bus, awaiting a doctor's appointment, or waiting for the car to get an oil change. Putting off a task makes it that much harder. Make "Do it now!" your motto. It may save your getting an ulcer.

5. BE ADJUSTABLE.

There are emergencies which demand that we adjust our time to meet the situation. It is called "situational management" in colleges of business. Accidents, crises in the lives of students, administrative demands, all call for an adjustable life-style. But that does not mean that you give up control of your time. It may mean after-school work or taking home some task that is pressing.

6. THE DANGER OF SAYING "YES"!

There are people who just can't say "No!" Can you? It is tempting to say "Yes" to many good causes or to volunteer for a committee. People, especially beginning teachers, forget that every time you appoint a committee, or are a member of a committee, you are spending money that is *time.* It is true that "time is money." And some school administrators seem not aware that each committee meeting is an expenditure of time *and* money. Be choosy in your commitments. People will respect your time if you respect it. The faculty coffee shop can be a useful place for exchange of information, or it can be a "goof-off" hangout for procrastinators. You can save worries by not being a victim of procrastination. Make time your friend by sticking to your schedule. Remember: YOU ARE THE ONE IN CHARGE!

7. MAKE YOUR DATE BOOK YOUR FRIEND!

Keeping a careful log or date book will help you know how you are spending your life energy. Think of life as spirit, mind, and body. It can be thought of as a triangle where you try to keep a balance of each. A pedant is a bore, a cultivated mind is a joy, and a healthy body is an absolute necessity. Keeping time on your appointments will give you a kind of freedom. You can know what is important and what is mostly a waste of time. "Killing time" is the worst kind of murder. And beginning teachers are establishing habits of time management that will prove useful throughout their professional careers.

8. LIST OBJECTIVES—IN WRITING!

Climbing the Grand Canyon begins with a first step; so it is with your professional growth. List your educational objectives and then stick by them. Do you want an advanced degree? Do you want an investment plan for retirement? Do you want to meet the right life-partner? Plan for it, make time for each, and prioritize. An annual checkup at the end of each academic year will keep you on target. Some objectives you will have accomplished, some will take a lesser priority, and some you may want to drop. If you know where you are going and why, you may get there. If you don't, you may be sure you will never get where you want to in life. You may want to review your objectives with an intimate friend. Input from an objective outsider may prove most valuable.

9. YOU CAN'T DO IT ALL—FARM IT OUT!

Don't be ashamed that you are not a walking encyclopedia. Beginning teachers need to learn to delegate. Again, let us stress that you use other teachers who are specialists; use community leaders who can enrich your classes with their specialties (a travel agent who has just returned from a foreign country may love to show his slides), students, some of whom have rich backgrounds to share, consultants in the system (art, music, drama, and speech). It is the wise beginning teacher who knows his/her forte and maximizes the strengths in teaching and minimizes his/her weaknesses. If you are a good storyteller, tell lots of stories! If you don't have a singing voice, call on the choir director to help. Everyone likes to have his talents recognized, so you will be more appreciated if you delegate, or farm out, some of the work. And look out! You may just end up in administration if you are good at it.

10. TIME FOR CONTINUING EDUCATION!

It was Alice in Wonderland who said, "I have to run just to stay in the same place." That is true of teachers, too. We have to practice continuing education and take time for it in our planning. James A. Michener was taking notes on the South Pacific Islands when he was in the navy while some others were playing cards or wasting time. Result: the book *Hawaii*. He was establishing learning habits which proved useful throughout his lifetime. The same is true of the beginning teacher.

You might make a list of the books you want to read in the next five years. Prioritize them and read the ones which will help you most in your new profession first of all. It will pay off. Set time aside for reading — pleasure reading, professional reading, and random reading. Waiting while in a physician's office can be utilized for random reading. Professional reading may pay off in correspondence courses, magazines in your field, or "new fields" — to open up horizons. Pleasure reading can be in form of novels, historical books, or humor. Much wisdom can be gained from Sam Levinson's book, *Everything But Money*. (He was a teacher, too.) Other books to enjoy would be Art Buchwald's (a witty journalist, really a philosopher), and Robert Muller's *Most of All They Gave Me Happiness,* a story of how he became a world citizen. Our reading can make us much more interesting persons, and we need broadly educated teachers. Another recommended book is Claude Coleman's, *We Need Whole Men, Not Splinters.*

So, how we use our time will determine what we become. And learning how to use time wisely is perhaps life's greatest lesson. By keeping the "time tips" before you, you can make time a friend, not an enemy.

QUESTIONS

1. List some techniques for improving your organization of your time.
2. Explain what is meant by prioritizing.
3. Where are some places where one can use time while waiting?
4. Suggest some books and/or authors which make for helpful reading.
5. What is the key to time management?

Chapter 19

ARE YOU COMMUNICATING?

Language is the indispensable mechanism of human life—of life such as ours that is molded, guided, enriched, and made possible by the accumulation of the *past* experience of members of our own species.[1]

Communication, whether we're talking about the sound waves of speech, the light waves bouncing off a printed page or the radio waves of broadcast speech, always involves at least two people: a sender and a receiver. And unless the sender and receiver are "tuned in" to one another, communication will be blocked. That is, if A is trying to convey information to B, his/her success will depend, not just on what he says and how he says it, but on how well B can understand what he's saying.[2]

DIFFERENCES IN VOCABULARY AND DIALECT

The extreme case, of course, is when A and B speak different languages. But the same principle applies, though to a lesser degree, if they speak different dialects of the same language. Here *some* communication will probably take place—but how much will depend on how different the dialects are. A may be saying in his dialect precisely what he means—yet B, speaking a different dialect, may receive only a blurred notion of what A is getting at.[3]

Or sometimes he may get a completely clear but wholly mistaken notion, as in the old story of the American woman in London who was shocked when a young Englishman told her, "I'll come over and knock you up when I get my screw." (American translation: "I'll come around and call on you when I get my pay.")[4]

The vocabulary of the English language is so extensive that only the most learned can know more than a small fraction of the total. But even the small fraction that most of us know gives us many alternatives in individual word choice. All of us have in our vocabularies various levels of diction, and most of us choose from these levels according to the circumstances confronting us.[5]

PRE-TEST EARLY IN THE YEAR

I learned dramatically the importance of this technique when I was a novice teacher. I had a group of seniors, and I was not many years older than they. I began my lectures immediately, and this group blandly sat staring at me smugly as if they dared me to teach them anything they did not already know. They were on the offensive, so to speak, and they had put me on the defensive. I was apprehensive as to whether or not I could relate to them, and I experienced some miserable beginning days. Then, perhaps by hearing a suggestion from a more experienced colleague, I decided to pretest. As I remember, this was a course in "Races and Nations," and I tested with such elementary questions as, "Who was Dr. Martin Luther King?" Their ignorance in this realm was abysmal. From that time forward, the class knew definitely that I was on the offensive and that I knew of their lack of knowledge on the subject.

TEACH: THEN RE-TEST

I took an education class in college in which all semester long the professor stressed and repeated mainly five simple points: Pre-test; Teach; Test; Re-teach; Re-test. In other words, constantly evaluate, and you will each time be surprised at what has been communicated or what has been misconstrued and not communicated. Then you must re-teach within the student's framework.

GIVE INSTRUCTIONS IN SPECIFIC WORDS AND NOT ABSTRACTIONS

Give specific instructions; then have the student repeat to you what instructions he understood.

Stuart Chase in his book THE TYRANNY OF WORDS stresses that every word should have a specific referent. That is, when you say "chair," what type of chair are you thinking of? When you say "Mother," is your student envisioning the same referent which you are? Obviously not. It is vastly important, then, for the instructor to discover within what framework a student is operating and to gear language carefully within the framework of the student.

When politicians talk, or when newspapers publish propaganda, the writing many times is in abstractions. What is meant by "equality"? Do you mean specifically that women should get equal pay with men? Or do you mean that all races have equal rights? What is meant by "patriotism"?

Do you mean fighting in a war, or do you mean refusing to fight for an unjust cause? Always ask, "What is the specific referrent?"

Another lesson I learned through experience in the classroom with different groupings of students was to use different words with different classes. Particularly is it best with the ones from ghetto areas to avoid certain words which to them have obscene connotations. Their guffaws and sneers can wreak havoc with discipline and bring discouragement to a teacher. Part of the learning process is difficult for a teacher who has been raised in a middle-class environment.

For the new teacher the language barrier can make or break a person. It takes time to learn what are the objectionable terms and what are the acceptable ones, and those often vary from class to class. Nevertheless, it is vitally important for one to become alert to the different patterns of speech.

It is not so much that you need to learn the language of the streets but only to know what terms or words to avoid which might have very different connotations to the group with whom you are working from what the words mean to you. You need, so far as possible, to operate within a framework where you will be understood, but, most of all, so that you will not be misunderstood.

KEY GANG VOCABULARY

■ **Banging** — Being involved in gang activities such as fighting or drug sales.

■ **Original gangster** — Hardcore gang members call themselves gangsters, an original gangster or O.G. It is a member with rank or seniority.

■ **Senior staff** — High-ranking gang member, sometimes used interchangeably with O.G.

■ **Homies, homeboys** — Fellow gang member, friend.

■ **Being jumped in or out** — Initiation to become a member of a gang or get out of a gang. Usually involves fighting members of the gang for a certain amount of time.

■ **Set** — Gang members who come from a particular locale and have given allegiance to a particular group.

red. Also called Pirus.

■ **Crips** — Also an L.A.-based black gang with membership in other states. Rival to Bloods. Color is generally blue.

■ **Show-by** — Display of weapons, usually used to intimidate.

■ **Colors** — Gangs are often identified by distinctive colors or color combinations of clothing, hats, bandannas, etc.

■ **Dressed down** — Wearing gang colors.

■ **Confederation** — Identification with a state or national confederation of gangs, such as Crips or Bloods.

■ **Signing** — Hand and arm signals and other types of body expressions used to identify with a specific gang or confederation. May be used to challenge a rival gang.

Used by permission of *Tribune Newspaper,* Sunday, May 3, 1992 (Bob Schuster).

■ **Bloods** — Los Angeles-based black gang with sets showing up in other states. White youth are beginning to claim membership in Blood sets, too. Color is generally

■ **Sagging** - Wearing pants low enough to make underclothes visible.

■ **'Hood** — Short for neighborhood.

KEY POLICE VOCABULARY

■ **Youth at risk** — Children ages 6 to 12 who live under socioeconomic conditions conducive to gang activity or dropping out of school.

■ **Hardcore** — Totally involved in a gang. Usually the leaders, these members often determine the gang's level of violence and other criminal activity. Often they are the most violent, streetwise and experienced members, and they are considered the most dangerous. Full-fledged gang members refer to themselves as gangsters.

■ **Associates** — Those associated with the gang for status and recognition. They wear the group's colors and attend social functions.

■ **Peripherals** — Usually the youngest members who move in and out on the basis of interest in the activities of the gang.

■ **Wannabes** — Those who are attempting to gain membership. They may try to prove themselves by committing some crime or act of violence.

■ **Gang incident** — Unit for classifying and reporting an event as a gang crime. The statistics become the basis for determining whether a gang problem exists in a particular area. A gang incident can be either gang-motivated or gang-related, depending on which description a police department uses. Gang-motivated is considered more accurate in describing a situation as a gang crime. It avoids the tendency to excessively label or stigmatize gang members.

■ **Gang-motivated** — An act that directly benefits the gang as a whole, such as a drive-by shooting or the seizure of a gang jacket.

■ **Gang-related** — An act that involves someone — witness, perpetrator or victim — who is identified as a gang member either by himself or others, regardless of the type of crime involved. Under this definition, the crime of a gang member who steals from a store, even though it had nothing to do with his gang membership, would be classified as a gang-related incident.

ENDNOTES

1. Hayakawa, S. I., *Language in Thought and Action,* New York, Harcourt, Brace, 1964, p. 13.
2, 3, and 4. Claiborne, *Saying What You Mean,* New York, W. W. Norton, 1986, p. 20.

QUESTIONS

1. Why is pre-testing a workable technique?
2. Why is continual evaluation necessary?
3. How can problems be avoided if a teacher learns how better to give instructions?
4. How are one's choice of words and the maintaining of class discipline related?

Chapter 20

SCHOOL IS—

SCHOOL IS:

When you've prepared a very special lesson and are in the middle of presenting it and the fire alarm rings for you to evacuate your class from the building.

When you've come to school with a bad headache and you have to sit at the desk and sweat out the morning.

When you count on your "A" student to make a special presentation at the Open House and the student calls in sick.

When it's the end of a long, hard week; then you learn that your evaluation was outstanding.

When you learn that the Mexican gang is going to fight off the clique of white students as soon as school is out that day.

When your teacher's report is due on Friday afternoon, and you've just been assigned one more extra-curricular sponsorship.

When you think your lesson didn't get across to the class, and one student calls out, "This is the best book I've ever read."

When your absentee report is due five minutes after the bell rings and your class is barely settled down.

When you were out late the night before, are less prepared than usual and the Administrative evaluator walks in to observe.

When a teenager has just told you that she's pregnant; then you hear that your class has placed first in academic honors.

When you've had a thorny session with a troubled student; then a colleague walks in to ask you out to dinner.

When the handsomest male teacher on campus has asked you to go out on Saturday night, and you'd already promised to sponsor a weekend school activity.

When your class has won a silver trophy for excellence; then you discover that one student has cheated.

When a pupil has just caused you a discipline problem; then a student with beaming face hands you a card signed, "You're the greatest!"

When there's camaraderie with your fellow instructors during coffee break time.

QUESTIONS

Write one paragraph pointing out the realism of a school teaching day.

Chapter 21

WHO ARE YOUR STUDENTS?

Who are these students of yours in a democracy? From where did their parents and grandparents come? Let's review briefly the composition of the "Melting Pot" of America and learn from what directions their ancestors came. If we take a look at their historical backgrounds, we will marvel that we communicate at all.

BLACKS

Blacks are the second largest racial group in the country. Provisional 1980 census figures showed 26,488,218 blacks living in the United States, about 12 percent of the total population of 226,504,825 (1980 Census of Population, 1981). Of these, roughly three-quarters live in urban areas, and about 47 percent live in the North. This is a significant shift from the 1940's, when roughly 80 percent of American blacks lived in the South and worked in agriculture.[1]

World War II saw an acceleration of the movement toward equality for blacks. The number of black officers in the armed services grew. President Roosevelt issued an executive order that forbade racial discrimination in defense industries and created the Fair Employment Practices Committee. The Supreme Court continued to hand down decisions favorable to blacks.[2]

Changes have continued since World War II. President Truman in 1947 established the Committee on Civil Rights, and the following year saw the publication of its significant report, TO SECURE THESE RIGHTS.

The armed services were integrated. Many states adopted fair employment practices laws. In 1954 the Supreme Court handed down its historic decisions regarding the inequality of separate educational facilities.[3]

The changing status of blacks could be seen by their prominence on Olympic teams and in radio, television, and the movies. Black novelists, poets, and artists were winning international acclaim, and black scholars began to receive appointments in leading universities. Their political power began to be used effectively, and the major parties vied for their vote. Big business became aware of their economic importance and began to compete for their patronage.[4]

However, today, despite decades of intensive political struggle as well as significant progress, social and economic equality still evades blacks; for example, the income of black families still averages only 59 percent that of whites and only 62 percent of the national average (*Money Income of Households in the United States: 1979, 1981*)—just 2 percent above Indians who have the lowest average income (Urban Institute, 1978). Most sociologists believe that this is the result of enduring prejudice directed against blacks.[5]

SPANISH

American English has borrowed more words from Spanish than from any other language, and is still borrowing them. There are hundreds of thousands of Mexicans living in the Southwest; 650,000 Puerto Ricans in New York City; and 100,000 Cubans in New Orleans, plus many hundred thousand more in the Miami area. It all started with the 16th Century Spanish explorers and conquistadors.[6]

Puerto Ricans have managed to pull slightly ahead of blacks in family income at 63 percent of the national average (Urban Institute, 1978). However, as of 1979, 38.8 percent of Puerto Ricans living on the mainland still were below the poverty level (*Statistical Abstract of the United States, 1980*).[7]

JEWS

The Jews who came to America never spoke Hebrew as their native language. Hebrew is used only in prayer and religious ceremonies. Thus from the first 23 Dutch Jews who came to New Amsterdam from Brazil in 1654, to the 2,500 Jews attending religious services in 1776 (mainly in such cities as New York, Philadelphia, Newport, Charleston, and Savannah), to the 200,000 German Jews who came to America between 1840 and 1860, Jewish immigrants influenced the American language by bringing the language of their native lands: English, German, Dutch, French, etc. Then between 1880 and 1910 almost 3 million Central and Eastern European Yiddish-speaking Jews came to America as part of that great wave of New Immigrants.[8]

FRENCH

The prairie, that great American grassland, was named by French explorers, trappers, and fur traders spilling west from the Mississippi and eastern Canada. The same French who first explored the prairie also gave us other words.[9]

Our language can tell us a lot about our history, and knowing that pupils may have vastly differing backgrounds from their ancestors should make a teacher recognize individual differences and have more understanding of their varying backgrounds.

SCOTCH-IRISH

The true Scotch-Irish were originally Lowland Scots Presbyterians (small farmers, cottagers, and, mainly, weavers) who had been settled by the English in the turbulent Northern Ireland counties, collectively called Ulster, to replace the rebellious Irish in the 1600's. Hating both the low-class Irish Catholics and the upperclass Church of England English landlords, and suffering from harassment by the British textile industry and a series of crop failure in the 1720's, these Scots who had lived in Ireland flocked to the American colonies. In fact, between 1730 and 1770 almost half of Ulster sailed to the New World and by 1776 one out of every seven colonists was Scotch-Irish.[10]

GERMANS

Since English is a Germanic language it has always been full of "German" words and word elements. A small trickle of Germans arrived in America after 1640, became a small flow around 1820, increased again around 1845 when the Potato Blight struck Germany almost as hard as it did Ireland, and became a flood after the German Revolution of 1848. In all, just under 7 million German immigrants have come to the U.S. since 1776.[11]

IRISH

It was the Irish Potato Famine of 1846—actually a widespread European potato famine caused by the potato blight—which sent the wave of Irish immigrants to America. By 1860 over 1½ million Irish immigrants were in America, the largest foreign-born group then in the country.[12]

WHITE ANGLO-SAXON PROTESTANTS

Of 222,300,000 Americans in 1978, 10,892,000 were of English, Scottish, or Welsh origin. These Americans of British origin are often grouped together as white Anglo-Saxon Protestants (WASPs). Although in terms of their numbers they are a minority within the total American population, they have been in America the longest (aside from Native Americans) and as a group have always had the greatest economic and political power in the country.[13]

ITALIANS

Few Italians immigrated to America until after 1865. Then over 5 million Italians came to the U.S. as part of the New Immigration. They usually settled in large northeastern cities, in sections soon called Little Italy.[14]

NATIVE AMERICANS

When the Pilgrims landed, there were a thousand unique Indian nations north of the Rio Grande, speaking 58 major languages.

OTHER PEOPLES

Between 1900 and 1920 alone 14½ million new immigrants came to America, averaging a million a year, 2,000 every day.[15]

More recently the constituency of many classrooms is composed of children and young people of parents from Mexico, Vietnam, China and Japan, Samoa, Thailand, Taiwan, European countries and the refugees from Ethiopia and other wartorn countries.

ENDNOTES

1. Tischler, Whitten, and Hunter, *Introduction to Sociology,* New York, 1983, p. 334.
2. Flexner, Stuart Berg, *I Hear America Talking,* New York, Van Nostrand Reinhold, 1976.
3, 4, 5, and 6. Tischler, pp. 335–336.
7. Flexner, p. 319.
8. Tischler, p. 337.
9. Flexner, pp. 279–280.
10. *Ibid.,* p. 314.
11. *Ibid.,* pp. 164–165.
12. *Ibid.,* p. 135.
13. Tischler, p. 331.

14. Flexner, p. 215.
15. Flexner, p. 193.

QUESTIONS

1. What evidence has there been regarding the changing status of the blacks in recent years?
2. How does the income of the black families compare with those of white families?
3. What group has the lowest average income?
4. What group has contributed the most words to our English language?
5. Who have wielded the greatest economic and political power in our country?
6. How great an immigrant population has America had to assimilate?
7. From what countries more recently have immigrants come?

Chapter 22

WHO ACTUALLY CONTROLS?

Sometimes teachers report to their classrooms day after day not knowing actually who has done the groundwork for setting the rules for
paying their salaries or who establishes educational philosophy and
policies within the system.

An instructor can function much more intelligently if he/she recognizes who actually controls. Hence, this chapter deals with some basic
structure undergirding the educational process.

THE STATE BOARD OF EDUCATION

The State Board of Education carries out functions regarding the type of
education the students within the state will receive, and the members
of the State Board are appointed by the Governor. It is obvious that when
a governor is of one political persuasion his viewpoint and philosophy
might well be influenced by his own orientation and political perspective which will no doubt be reflected in his appointments.

THE STATE SUPERINTENDENT OF PUBLIC INSTRUCTION

Known by a number of different titles, the chief school administrator
is the overall supervisor of the public school system in every state. Most
often this officer is known as the Superintendent of Public Instruction
or the Commissioner of Education. He or she usually shares authority
with the State Board of Education.[1]

The voters still choose the chief school officer in 18 states, in most
cases on a nonpartisan basis. The post is filled by the governor in but 8
states, and by the Board in the other 24.[2]

The method by which the state superintendent is selected sometimes
varies, however.[3]

If the governor should be of one political party and the State Superintendent of another, there could be definite conflicts within the structure.
Hence it is vitally incumbent upon the electorate in a democracy to be
well informed as to the attitudes of the governor regarding his commit-

ment toward how much financing the educational program within the state will receive.

There are a vast number of other state agencies which have some influence on various aspects of the school systems in a state. In order to carry out certain legislative and constitutional provisions about education, any number of other boards of control exist, including controlling boards for higher education, vocational education, tenure, retirement, and similar activities. These are all in addition to a state board of education, which exists to determine policies that are then implemented by the state education agency. There are a variety of agencies concerned with budgeting, accounting, building standards, health, school lunches, library services, civil defense, and myriad other activities in which the schools, along with many other of the public welfare-delivery systems, engage. In short, while the local school system is often viewed as an autonomous unit, it is subject to the controls and impingements from an array of other legally established community and state agencies.[4]

THE STATE LEGISLATURE

Who determines how much shall be allotted yearly for education and for schools within the state? The State Legislature. Hence, here again the political climate can set the tone for the allotment of funds for education. In other words, your salary within your school situation is highly dependent upon how the Legislature votes regarding support for educational programs.

A sad example of voting against funds for education was the passage of Proposition 13 in California which saved the taxpayers large amounts on their property taxes but was a devastating move regarding funds for education.

Thus if a teacher is vitally interested in the progress of education within her/his state, it behooves those in the profession to be in close contact with the issues which are brought up each session in the Legislature and to make themselves heard (often through professional organizations) and to lobby their Legislative representatives. Local newspapers as a rule carry the notice of times certain bills are heard and/or voted on during a legislative session, and there is always at the front desk in the State Capitol building information regarding what is happening during the legislative session.

THE LOCAL BOARD OF EDUCATION

Who are they? These are the people, whether or not you realize it, who hired you, voted on how much salary you would receive, and set the policies regarding how forward-looking and progressive, or how regressive, your school system would be regarding modern methods and other issues. They have the final authority regarding whether or not a teacher should be retained or fired. They set policy concerning many matters within the District.

In rural communities, schools — and teachers' lives — tend to be strongly dominated by local school boards. Not only do those boards have strong opinions about what teachers should and shouldn't do (both in and out of the classroom), but they consider themselves independent, even in relationship to government rules and regulations. Teachers in small rural communities, more than in other types of situations, may be subject to a great degree of personal and professional scrutiny.[5]

HOW DO LOCAL SCHOOL BOARD MEMBERS GET THEIR POSITIONS?

The members of the local Board of Education are elected by the voters within the particular community. Despite the fact that often voter turn-out for school elections is deplorably small, yet the importance of Board elections cannot be over-emphasized.

In one instance a Board member was elected who had no more than a 5th grade education, and the principal of that school had him attend many workshops to broaden his educational scope. However, that Board member continued to cause difficulty within the school because of the narrowness of his vision.

In another instance a Board that had several members on it who were college graduates was able to provide excellent leadership within the community. Which Board members do you think would be apt to pay higher teachers' salaries, who would better understand teacher objectives, and who would be able better to help educate the young people of their community?

It is incumbent upon the conscientious teacher to help enlighten the public regarding the vital importance of School Board elections, partly for the good of the community and partly for that teacher's own self-preservation.[6]

A CHECKLIST FOR SCHOOL BOARDS

Boards of education are responsible for making policy and serving the public's interest in the schools. Is your board a good one? Good school boards are characterized by:

1. Concern for the education and equal opportunity for all children at all grade levels.
2. An orientation toward resolving problems, not placing blame.
3. Representing the whole community's interests, not particular groups or individuals, or individual issues.
4. Maintaining their policy-making role and not getting involved in day-to-day administration.
5. No conflicts of interest or other indiscretions which can compromise their integrity.
6. An open-mindedness to new approaches or change and a willingness to learn.
7. Making decisions on facts, not opinions, perceptions or prejudice.
8. Keeping informed about instructional and management issues.
9. Holding administrators accountable for effective leadership and efficient management procedures.
10. Supporting the teaching and administrative staff and treating them as professionals.[7]

School Board meetings are open to the public, and agendas should be posted so that the citizens might know the forthcoming issues. If there are issues which directly affect the faculty, it is well for the faculty to have representation at the Board meeting.

BOND ISSUES AND TAX ELECTIONS

Many times teachers as well as the public are not aware of the fact that there is a difference between a bond election and a tax election. Perhaps a community has had a bond election, and then when a tax election is needed, the public may react by feeling that funds for schools have already been voted.

When the public votes in a tax election, obviously they are voting for an increase in their property taxes to support the schools and to increase teachers' salaries in many cases.

To vote money for a bond election is to grant the Board authority to float bonds often for new buildings and this money cannot be used for salaries.

By law, some funds raised for specific purposes cannot be used for other purposes. If a teacher's salary, or those of her colleagues, is at stake, it behooves the teacher to learn how to lobby one's legislators and/or the Legislature.

ENDNOTES

1. McClenaghan, Wm. A., *Magruder's American Government,* Boston, Allyn & Bacon, Boston, 1983, p. 551.
2. *Ibid.,* p. 551.
3 and 4. Ubben, Gerald C. and Hughes, Larry W., *The Principal,* Boston, Allyn & Bacon, 1987, pp. 72 and 73.
5. *Ibid.,* p. 73.
6. Farber, Barry A. *Crisis in Education,* San Francisco, Jossey-Bass, 1991, pp. 260–261.
7. Goens, Dr. George A. and Clover, Dr. Sharon I. R., *Getting the Most From the Public Schools,* Florida, Pineapple Press, 1987, p. 25.

QUESTIONS

1. What is the objective of the Board of Education?
2. How do individuals get their positions on the State Board of Education?
3. What is the function of the State Superintendent of Public Instruction?
4. How does the State Superintendent get his/her position?
5. Why is it important for a teacher to know what is happening in the State Legislature?
6. What influence on your position does the local Board of Education have? How will it help you if you are alert to the Board's agenda?
7. How do members of the local Board of Education get their positions?
8. Why is it important for a teacher to know what is happening at election time regarding the local Board of Education?
9. What are some qualities which are desirable in an effective school board?
10. What is a bond election and for what do the school monies go if school bonds are passed?
11. How does a bond election differ from a tax election? For what do monies go that are voted in a regular tax election?

Chapter 23

WHAT DOES YOUR PRINCIPAL DO?

Sometimes teachers have the erroneous idea that principals and/or administrators sit in their offices all day and do very little. Particularly if a school is running smoothly, it may appear that the machinery is so well-oiled that there is not much need for administrators.

It is like the husband who asked his wife what she did at home all day when he was gone, so she decided one day just not to do her regular housework. When the husband came home that evening, the beds were unmade, the dishes not done, no dinner on the table, the children were in dirty clothes, and the whole house was in general disarray. When he asked what in the world had happened, she said, "Well, you asked what I do all day, so I decided today not to do it. Now, can you tell?"

Likewise the work of administrators often may not be evident, but the principal is the key to the entire school situation. Teachers in a smooth-running school might not realize the advance planning which has taken place or the night meetings of work on school budgets.

Let us deal briefly with the work of the principal. What are the functions which comprise the principalship? Basically, there are five main functions. These functions include:

(1) staffing and personnel development
(2) pupil personnel services
(3) program development
(4) resource procurement and building management (budgeting and maintenance)
(5) school, community, faculty and board relations[1]

I. STAFFING AND PERSONNEL DEVELOPMENT

Under the principal's aegis comes responsibility of scheduling staff and students, team planning, and organizing the school instruction. Supervision and evaluation of staff also are included, so that responsibility of hiring and termination are the principal's.

II. PUPIL PERSONNEL SERVICES

Setting goals, developing an environment conducive to learning, and student control are all influenced by the philosophy of the main administrator.[2]

III. PROGRAM DEVELOPMENT

It is incumbent upon the principal to implement the staff's programs, organize the school curriculum, and develop leadership.[3]

IV. RESOURCE PROCUREMENT AND BUILDING MANAGEMENT (BUDGETING AND MAINTENANCE)

Submitting a yearly budget to the Board of Education, managing the financial resources, supplies and equipment, plus care of the school plant enlist the time of the principal. Properly accounting for the available funds is his responsibility, and keeping a good school environment and a well-kept school building.[4]

V. SCHOOL-COMMUNITY RELATIONS

He/she must not only manage the school but must relate well to members of the teaching staff, the Board of Education, the parents, and alumni within the community.[5]

VI. KNOWLEDGE OF LEGAL PRINCIPLES

One more function might be added, and that is that he/she must have a good working knowledge about the legal principles governing the operation of the school. He/she must keep alerted as to the state and federal legislation which will affect the school situation.

A good principal, as far as teachers are concerned, is himself or herself a strong, autonomous person who treats the teaching staff as professionally independent.[6]

Without doubt, teachers will experience greater work satisfaction and higher morale when they are viewed by their principal as the professionals which they perceive themselves to be. Correspondingly, principals of the schools perceived by teachers to be "more satisfying" are more likely to perceive their teaching staff as competent professionals than are principals of a "less satisfying" school.[7]

Circumstances expedite or detract from the ability of both teachers and principals to perform at high levels and have satisfying work, and some of these circumstances are on the fringes of or outside of their span of control.[8]

School officials who hope to facilitate frequent and purposeful exchange among staff must ensure that preparation periods are productively aligned, classrooms are arranged to permit frequent interaction, schools are not disrupted by frequent staffing changes, and substitutes are available when teachers leave their students to observe or work with their peers.

School officials must do what they can to promote cooperation rather than competition while recognizing the limits of administrative control and genuinely respecting teachers for their expertise.[9]

Whatever support administrators provide, teachers themselves must ultimately take responsibility for collaboration.[10]

WHAT ARE QUALITIES OF A GOOD PRINCIPAL?

A 1979 University of Indiana review of 59 case studies of exceptionally successful urban schools (most conducted between 1971 and 1974) found that the most frequently reported variables were the leadership style of the school's principal.

Specifically, these studies suggest these qualities of effective principals:

1—**They take strong initiative in identifying and articulating goals and priorities for their schools.** They run their schools rather than allowing them to operate by force of habit. They hold themselves and their staff members personally accountable for student achievement in the basic skills. They will not accept excuses, however sympathetic they may be to students' problems.[11]

2—**They understand the school's educational program inside out.** They are "instructional leaders" versus "administrative leaders." They often have strong backgrounds in reading instruction, or they have found someone else who can provide direction in this area. Their first priority is instruction, and they communicate this to their staff.[12]

3—**They spend about half their time in the school's halls and classrooms.** They are not afraid of working directly with teachers. They are "high visibility" leaders, rather than ones who spend most of their time in their offices. They might not be aware of everything that's going on in their schools at all times, but they have created that impression in the minds of their staff and students.[13]

4—**They attempt to handpick their staffs** despite constraints from teachers' unions and school system bureaucracies. They put direct pressure on incompetent teachers to leave, and they find ways to award excellent teachers with greater responsibilities and recognition.[14]

5—They set a consistent tone of high expectations for their staffs and their students. This works both ways: what staff and students can expect from the principal and what the principal expects from them. These kinds of principals are most likely assertive disciplinarians, creating a school climate in which instruction can flourish.[15]

They care more about their schools' academic progress than human relations or informal, collegial relationships with their staff members. They are not afraid to be disliked.

Hence we see that the administrator's days, and often evenings, are involved with staffing and personnel development, with pupil personnel services, with program development, with resource procurement and building management, with budgeting and maintenance, and with relationships with school, community, faculty, and board.

YOU KNOW YOU'RE AN ELEMENTARY PRINCIPAL WHEN...*

Cliff Schadler

You know you're an elementary principal when...

... you get more Valentines than anyone else in the building.
... the school's boiler becomes part of your daily life.
... your heart skips a few beats when the superintendent calls.
... everyone comes to you for answers to difficult questions.
... you receive 25 leg hugs when you visit the kindergarten.
... kids yell out your name at the supermarket.
... you spend the most time on problems that least affect student learning.
... you find yourself with four meetings scheduled on the same day at the same time.
... you're excited about getting back to school and it's only the first week of August.
... a drooping dandelion from a student means as much to you as a bouquet from anyone else.

But can you tell me why...

... phones always ring within 12 seconds after the secretary leaves the office.
... the most physically affectionate students are the ones who have head lice.
... a sick student always throws up three steps short of the front door.
... a flying snowball on the playground always hones in on the nearest eye.

---

*From *The Principal* magazine, Vol. 71, # 4, March, 1992, page 60.

... when the west side of the building is too hot, the east side is too cold.

... enrollment is always 24 over or under the projected number.

... any schedule, after being corrected, reviewed, and revised, will always contain at least two conflicts.

... you will be short one box of masking tape, no matter how carefully you budget for supplies.

... the staff member who lives closest to school is always the last to arrive.

... those who run fastest in the hallways are slowest in the classroom.

... the copy machine will always run out of paper when you're in a hurry.

... accidents always occur after the nurse has gone.

... the most dangerous playground equipment is always the most popular.

... the child who causes the most problems never gets sick.

... the boiler always fails on the coldest day of the year.

... the new curriculum never solves all the problems you thought it would.

... more green beans end up in the garbage can after lunch than in children's stomachs.

... your problem students always seem to ride with your problem bus driver.

... the longest PTA meetings always have the shortest agendas.

... the last shipment of student-purchased paperbacks always arrives the day after the school year ends.

But it never hurts for a principal to ...

... tell the staff that you value their opinions.

... ask a teacher, "How's everything? Can I help?"

... spend a few minutes on the playground with kids.

... say "I goofed"—even when you know you're right.

... listen politely to an irate parent.

... share with other principals what you have learned.

... take time to empathize with a troubled child.

... send thank-you notes to moms who bake birthday cakes.

... tell your secretary how much you appreciate her.

... shorten a dull staff meeting.

... go a whole week without using the intercom.

... eat lunch in the cafeteria with the kids.

... call parents to say something positive about their child.

... say, "Darned if I know, but I'll find out."

... say, "Honey, I'll be home right after school"—and mean it.

ENDNOTES

1. Ubben, Gerald C. and Hughes, Larry W., *The Principal,* Boston, Allyn and Bacon, 1987, p. 6.
2. *Ibid.,* p. 119.

3. Chubb, John E. and Moe, Terry M., *Politics, Markets, and America's Schools*, Washington, DC, The Brookings Institution, 1990, p. 152.
4. Ubbens and Hughes, *The Principal*, p. 340.
5. *Ibid.*, p. 6.
6. Goodlad, John I., *A Place Called School*, New York, McGraw Hill, 1983, p. 179.
7. Johnson, Susan Moore, *Teachers At Work*, New York, Basic Books, 1990, pp. 178–179.
8. Benjamin, Robert, *Making Schools Work*, New York, Continuum, 1981, p. 113.
9. *Ibid.*, p. 113.
10. *Ibid.*, pp. 113–114.
11. *Ibid.*, p. 114.
12. *Ibid.*, p. 114.
13. Schadler, Cliff, *The Principal Magazine*, New York, Yeshiva Day-Schools, Vol. 71:4, 1992, p. 60.

QUESTIONS

1. What responsibility does the principal have regarding staffing?
2. How does the philosophy of the principal relate to student control?
3. What authority can principals wield in program control?
4. Why must a principal be a good business manager?
5. How does a principal's philosophy regarding school maintenance affect discipline?
6. What is meant by a "high visibility" principal?
7. What might happen if a school principal does not keep alert of current state and federal legislation which affects education?
8. What are some characteristics of good principals?

Chapter 24

WHAT WILL BE A TYPICAL DAY?

In applying for any job, you would no doubt ask what kind of day you would be facing when you're working and what your typical day might be like.

Let us peek through the door of the typical schoolhouse and see what kind of day a teacher might well expect.

CLASS SCHEDULE

Let us begin with the day of the secondary school teacher. In most cases, that instructor would be assigned five classes of 25 or 30 students per class. Hopefully, that would include two separate preparations. That is, you might expect to teach two classes of one subject or of one type of grouping of students plus three classes of another phase of that subject with different groupings of students. Your class load, then, would consist of approximately 125 to 150 pupils each day.

Sometimes secondary teachers who have families feel that they are poorly paid to the extent that they assume "moonlighting" jobs—that is, an extra job after the day's work—to make ends meet. That, however, is not the norm.

Reporting to class and correcting papers for your class load does not include the total responsibility. As a rule, the instructor will also be assigned extra duties. In high school that might be either chaperoning a weekend dance or helping monitor a sports event. If one likes the teenagers and enters into their activities, one does not necessarily feel that these are onerous tasks because there is a certain amount of enjoyment in working along with the students in their activities. There are advantages in getting better acquainted with them and their interests and seeing them in a different milieu than in just the classroom situation.

In the case of the elementary teacher, the special assignments might be supervising children as they board the school bus, supervision in the hall, or cafeteria supervision as well as other types of out-of-class duty.

An instructor also gets involved in parent conferences, in Parent-Teachers' Association meetings, and in counseling sessions with students and with their parents.

There is no limit as to how much a conscientious instructor can become involved in community activities, particularly if one is teaching at the community college level where the philosophy is that one is training students to upgrade local community involvement and make for better citizenship on the part of students.

You probably will develop the habit of arriving at school early before class and checking in your mailbox regarding what news there will be regarding the events of the day. Many high schools have a daily news bulletin which you'll find there and which can be read to the students so that they, too, know what kind of a day to anticipate.

PREP PERIODS

While there are usually only a few minutes between classes, much of which is often consumed with questions from students, yet you'll welcome the one free period which you can utilize as a preparation period. Free? Not really. As a new teacher you might feel tempted to use that time for some socializing with other faculty who have the same type of schedule or asking questions of them regarding the school routine. That, of course, is vital and has its place. Before long, however, you'll discover that the period is most necessary not only for paper correcting but for xeroxing materials, ordering audio-visual equipment, preparing assignment sheets, and the like. If that period is not utilized to the fullest, one no doubt will find oneself carrying home papers to be corrected or needing to do preparation reading or other tasks into the evening or before morning classes.

Hence, the work of the teacher is structured to the point that there is little time to waste. The compensating factors are that *if* one enjoys the teaching day and the progress, hopefully, being shown by working with students, the pressures of the teaching load are more rewarding than burdensome.

EXTRA-CURRICULAR CAN BE FUN

Accompanying the academic pursuits are the times of release provided by the social life of the school. Football games, dances, school socials, teachers' conventions—all provide times of sociability and fellowship with students and faculty alike.

The interaction between teachers and students as well as between teachers and fellow faculty members makes the work of the profession provide many special joys and experiences which a teacher who has chosen the profession finds most rewarding.

Balance the seeming difficulties of some of the pressures with the opportunities to relax and enjoy activities along with students who have spirit and enthusiasm. You'll be making lasting friendships and feel it a privilege to relate to fellow colleagues who are educated in many skills and disciplines.

SUMMER VACATIONS?

Of course you have summer vacations to anticipate. So thinks the public, but are you sure? Usually a teacher must attend summer school classes either to maintain or update the teaching credential. If one is fortunate enough to be in a district where travel counts as "professional growth," one can look forward to a summer of travel. In either case, if you are a person who likes to learn continually, you should enjoy the continued occupation with educational advancement. However, don't be misled with the impression which many of the public have—that teachers have three full months of freedom from classroom demands. Sometimes that is true, but usually teachers become involved in the summers with interesting projects which will better prepare them for their future years of teaching.

AN EXAMPLE OF CONTINUED ACTIVITY INTEREST

Lewis Arnold, Antelope Valley (California) Division of California Teachers, retired in June, 1990 after 33 years in the Antelope Valley Union High School District. He was a former top athlete, coach, and teacher in the Math Department of the four high schools in the district.

Since retirement, Lew and his wife, Pat, have been competing in Country Western dancing. Their competitive activities have taken them all over the United States, as they compete against couples of all ages from all over the U.S., even Hawaii. Their skills have earned them many championships in the various categories of Country Western dance. At last count, they have won about 200 prizes and trophies. Their favorite is the "Spirit of Country" award. The trophy was awarded the couple who best exemplified feelings of warmth, friendliness, and upbeat attitudes.

"We hope to win the world title in the senior divisions," Pat Arnold said. "Although we have beaten the younger couples, we're not out for anyone's throat. We're here just to have a good time. And I think everyone else in this form of dancing act as though they are in one big family."

The Lewises have been invited to dance exhibitions for many different groups including State Assemblymen and famous Country Music stars. They are now instructing in Country Western Dance and coaching another couple for competition. They hope eventually to begin judging and teaching in a studio setting.

Although the Lewises are now retired, Lew and his wife, Pat, are the kind of people one meets during extra-curricular assignments in high school activities. There is great fun and fellowship on high school faculties and there are many talented and skilled people with whom it is a privilege to be associated and to get to know. Extra-curricular activities in school functions can often be a joy.

QUESTIONS

1. What type of class load would a high school instructor normally be assigned?
2. What are some extra-duty assignments a high school teacher may expect to get?
3. What extra jobs might the elementary teacher expect to have?
4. How might one's attitude toward extra-curricular assignments influence how one likes one's job?

Chapter 25

WHAT IS YOUR IMAGE OF TEENAGERS?

I worked with approximately 150 teenagers per day for many years and have met every variety, from the rebellious, surly delinquent to the affable, conscientious "A"-student type. When class elections are held, whom do they nominate, and who in turn gets elected? Is it the teenager who is discourteous and rude to his teachers, his parents, or his peers, or is it the teenager who keeps his grades up to par, mixes well with his peers, and remembers manners he learned at home? It is the latter type who wins every time and not the noisy attention-getter who vies for popularity.

Our student council, at one time which was composed of about fifteen representatives elected by the student body, was composed, not of Elvis Presley types, not of the kind who has the latest color streak in his forelock, not of the rock singer or the hot-rod fan. Whom do the students themselves elect to office? The manly football player, the neatly-dressed girl with the well-shampooed hair who rates well enough to be in the Scholarship Federation.

These are not standards which we alone set for the young people. These are the types of young people they admire. This is not true only of one school alone but could be multiplied as being typical of schools throughout the country I would venture. This is the image they care to create when they select their "Betty Blade" or "Bobby Blade"—or whatever the term might be which represents the most popular, well-liked student.

Parents who rate "tops" with them and teachers whose autographs they seek on their last school day are not necessarily the ones who have learned the "cha-cha" or have learned to sling the terms "dig," "awesome," "cool" or other teen-age jargon. These types of parents and teachers they often consider as immature and adolescent themselves. When left to choose a teacher of their choice or a parent or speaker of their choice, whom do they select? Someone who listens to them, someone who is interested in their problems, someone who himself is mature, integrated, and of course has other qualities of integration, including a sense of humor and an alert mind.

People are inclined to live up to an image which they are given. We portray certain images of "father" and "mother" and expect and encourage our children to adapt their behavior to fit into the pattern we create of the image of a benevolent father, a kindly, sympathetic mother, thus expecting a certain type of character after the fashion of that which we create in our minds.

But what image do we create of our teenagers? Time after time I hear lectures, speeches, and read newspaper articles regarding the "delinquent teenager," the confused, unhappy teen boy or the rebellious, impertinent young teen girl. Time after time we seem to impress upon the minds of impressionable youth the fact that when they progress from the elementary school into the middle school, then reaching teenage, that expected patterns and different types of behavioral characteristics are expected of them.

"Oh, you know how teenagers are." "The telephone was tied up last night because my daughter was hanging on the phone." "Susie talks back to me now since she's become a teenager. I can't control her anymore." "Teenagers are apt to be delinquent, you know." These are remarks I constantly hear. However there are as many different types of teenagers as there are adults.

If it is true that children and young people live up to what's expected of them, or are apt to, it's also true that when we constantly repeat remarks like the above, the teenager must begin to feel that something is abnormal with him if he isn't living up to the image which is projected of him.

What standards do teenagers create for themselves?

When I taught at Palm Springs High in California some of my highest achieving teenagers said to me, "Why do some people think that we like that rock and roll music? Some of us would much prefer some of the semi-classical or classical music. Sometimes adults insult our intelligence."

Most college-trained parents are extremely conscious of the fact that our psychologists have pointed out to us that teenagers are experiencing a difficult time, that physical changes make them erratic, irresponsible, that one minute they act adult and the next act like children. Is this any more reason to treat them as if we were afraid of their responses, their approval, their reactions? Parents who are strict and understanding and compassionate with elementary children sometimes talk to me about teenagers as though they were suddenly afraid of their own children, as though they were afraid to give them the security, the understanding, the strictness which they so want, even as they wanted it when they were younger. Parents, too, many times are experiencing physical difficulties, middle-age crises or erratic behavior, but do we suddenly treat them as strangers? No, we attempt to give them more security, more attention, and more understanding without being prying or overpossessive.

One year I asked my classes to write a paragraph regarding their ideas of the ideal teenager. The teenage boys were to write about "What I Like in a Teenage Girl." The girls, in turn, wrote of their conception of an ideal teenage boy. What were the results? You probably have already guessed that the boys stated that they did not like "loud-mouthed, disrespectful girls," that they liked a girl whom they would be proud to introduce to their parents; the girls wrote similarly that they liked a boy of whom they could be proud, one with manners, who had self-respect and individuality.

Likewise, a survey conducted in one of our schools in connection with orientation of new pupils included questions regarding parents and teachers they admired. The consensus of opinion was that they disliked parents who were either too permissive or too strict; they wanted certain boundaries drawn, and they respected those who drew them.

Many parents point out that delinquency among teenagers is at such an all-time high they are almost afraid to see what happens to their own children when they go through the crucial teenage years. Granted, delinquency rates are extremely high. Granted, we are experiencing the after-math of our embroilment in horrible wars. But look at the adult crime rate. Does this mean that we expect the major adult groups within our society to have the characteristics of criminals, to continually hear the image held up to them of disorganization, mental illness, and criminality? Newspapers, TV, and radio capitalize on crime stories of both adults and teenagers as attention-getting devices for the sale of their products.

So I plead with adults, and particularly with teachers, "Let's not expect inferior behavior of our teenagers or present to them an image that is less than that of excellence"—those teenagers who are so full of idealism, enthusiasm, creativity, and potential for the great dreams of the future, those who admire the pioneers of old when they are properly presented to them, those who search for the best in life if it is revealed to them.

Let us remember that God created parents and teachers for a purpose, that this purpose is to guide, direct (subtly and wisely), be devoted themselves to the highest and finest, and to give control when and where needed. Only then, as the twig has been bent, will it be able to grow strong and straight and true. If it were not so, parents and teachers would be superfluous, which is the mistaken position some adults take. So—Let's alter our image of our teenagers.

QUESTIONS

1. Why is it unfair to stereotype teenagers?
2. How may it influence young people if they are presented with a kind of stereotype?
3. What kind of peers do many teenagers often actually admire?

Chapter 26

USE THE COMPUTER

M ore and more the computer is a necessary part of our daily lives. When computers were first introduced, some people were intimidated by them. It is imperative in the modern world, however, to conquer any fear which one might have regarding the use of computers. Much of the time a teacher's routine tasks can be reduced with the use of electronic equipment and her/his time increased for individual attention to the needs of students.

When young people are graduated from high school in future years, learning the skills related to use of the computer will no doubt be a "must." The sales of computers have increased phenomenally in recent years, and people are becoming more and more aware of the value of computerizing a great variety of tasks.

CLASS MATERIALS

There are ways to produce attractive and eye-catching class materials with a computer.

BULLETIN BOARDS

Utilize the computer to make effective bulletin board displays.

STUDENT NEWSPAPERS

One can make the layout for a fairly professional looking student newspaper.

RECORD KEEPING

A computer spreadsheet on the computer can be useful as a record keeping device. What is a spreadsheet? It is an arrangement of rows and columns in which data may be stored and manipulated. Spreadsheets are a major form of software, with word processing and data bases as productivity tools. These were developed to cope with often time-consuming financial calculations but have found wide usage in other situations as well.[1] Once a spreadsheet is set up, it can be quickly changed with additional data being added or data facts deleted.

Besides record keeping, calculation worksheets can be done on the computer.

GRADE AVERAGING AND GRADE BOOKS

Grade books can be kept electronically and grade averages calculated. Since teachers often spend long hours averaging and recording grades, a computer can greatly reduce the time required if one learns to average grades on the computer. Also, a Grade Point Average Program which converts letter grades to numeric grades can save time.

CLASS LISTS

Using the computer to list the names of students, their addresses, their telephone numbers plus an emergency phone number, can expedite the process of having to copy such a class list.

TESTS AND QUIZZES

Tests may be given students through computer testing. Both multiple-choice tests and true-false tests can be taken on the computer. The questions are displayed one at a time until the student has taken all statements. Then a message will appear on the screen telling the student that the test is over. The student after that should press the space bar so that the number correct, the number incorrect, and the score will appear on the screen.

FILING

Of all the computer skills that students may gain, working with electronic filing systems may be one of the skills which students will find most useful for years to come.

WRITING AND EDITING

The word processor has greatly diminished the work of editing. A teacher can easily secure an inexpensive word processor which will greatly facilitate the writing process.

USE IN MANY DISCIPLINES

The computer can be used in spelling practice, in English, Reading, and Math. Many applications of the computer can be made in the

Science laboratory and classroom. In fields of Social Studies (especially Psychology and Sociology), where there is statistical data used, the computer can provide valuable help.

PERSONAL USE

For a teacher's personal files, one can develop a program for an appointment calendar to help keep track of appointments, conferences, or commitments one has made.

PERSONAL BUDGETING

Another helpful use would be a program to list detailed records of tax deductible expenses.

At the end of this chapter is a bibliography of some books to help a teacher in knowing types of programs in which a microcomputer in the classroom can prove most helpful.

Learn the functions of the computer and how to best utilize it, and you can save hours of your time. The usefulness of the computer, however, is dependent upon the teacher's creativity.

For further information about the use of computers, consult the following textbooks:

Bitter and Camuse, *Using a Microcomputer in the Classroom,* Englewood Cliffs, New Jersey, Prentice-Hall, 1988.

Bullough, Robert V., Sr. and Beatty, LaMond F., *Classroom Applications of Microcomputers,* New York, Macmillan, 1991.

Hayes, Jeanne, *Microcomputer & VCR Usage in Schools,* Denver, Colorado, Quality Education Data, 1988.

Lockard, Abrams, & Many, *Microcomputers for Educators,* Boston, Northern Illinois University, Little, Brown, 1987.

Maffei, Anthony C., Ph.D., *Classroom Computers,* New York, Human Sciences Press, 1986.

McRae, Jim, *101 Programs for the Classroom,* Blue Ridge Summit, PA., Tab Books, 1985.

Siegel, Martin A., and Davis, Dennis M., *Understanding Computer-Based Education,* New York, Random House, 1986.[2]

ENDNOTES

1. Lockard, Abrams, and Many, *Microcomputers for Educators,* Boston, 1987, p. 101.
2. *Ibid.,* p. 80.

QUESTIONS

1. How significant is it to know how to use the computer?
2. In what specific ways can a computer make life easier for an instructor?
3. List some special areas where developing computer skills can be utilized.
4. What are some courses in which use of the computer can be especially helpful?
5. How can knowing how to efficiently use the computer help in some of a teacher's personal tasks?

Chapter 27

TOMORROW'S TECHNOLOGY

Only a small number of schools nation-wide have gone wholeheartedly into high-technology education, but more and more schools are eyeing the field and sallying forth.

One measure of computer processing power is a MIP, for millions of instructions per second. Some of the personal computers used in businesses have about 20 MIPs as against educational computers' measly one, and 100-MIP personal computers are expected in a few years.[1]

The physical form of computers is also evolving, with notebook and hand-held computers becoming more common. Eventually, computers may be integrated into every student's and teacher's desk top. More likely, the computer's decreasing size and weight will enable students or teachers to travel from class to class with their own personal information devices.

Notebook computers—battery-powered computers the size of a stack of typing paper, or smaller—can store as much as 60 megabytes (60 million characters of data) in a magnetic hard disk the size of a cigarette pack. That's the equivalent of about 30,000 book pages of text information. Researchers say that in a few years, notebook computers may store hundreds of megabytes of data on rewriteable optical disks, which resemble audio compact disks. And they may be able to tap huge pools of information by plugging into a school's network as easily as one would plug a telephone into an outlet, or by using cellular and radio-frequency modems.[2]

A few years ago at Hill View Elementary in St. Lake City, Utah, the Administration and teachers decided to do something about apathy toward geography. Since children generally learn what the adults around them value, the principal decided to initiate a program that would educate the teachers and parents to think geographically. For the price of $100 modem, they discovered a way to bring the whole world to the children.[3]

Since 1988, they have used that modem to participate in a unique global electronic information service aptly dubbed "World Classroom," which links schools all over the world. GTE Directories, which developed World Classroom, invited the school to be one of five schools in the United States to pilot the program and paid the time charges for the students and teachers to telecommunicate via satellite.

World Classroom, which now includes 200 schools worldwide, is an interdisciplinary curriculum and information service that uses computers, phone lines, and modems to allow teachers and students around the world to share ideas and resources on mutual projects and current events. It is, in effect, a global electronic mail (e-mail) network. The program covers much more than geography. History and social studies have now become more interesting, and the children supplement their language arts studies by sending letters and journals via e-mail to fellow students in England, Holland, the Soviet Union, and throughout the United States.[4]

A LESSON IN HISTORY

A wonderful example of how the program has opened the children's eyes to the world around them occurred recently when the fourth graders began an e-mail correspondence with the fourth graders of Warmbrook Elementary in Chapel-en-le-Frith, Derbyshire, England.

The English students asked the kids here how old Salt Lake City is. Proudly, they answered, "Salt Lake City is very old. It was first settled in 1847! How old is your town of Chapel-en-le-Frith?"

Back via satellite came the reply: "Chapel-en-le-Frith was settled by the Normans. The name means "chapel in the forest." The chapel our town was built around was constructed in 1225".

Students were completely dismayed. Elementary children, being normally egocentric and ethnocentric at this stage in their cognitive development, think the world revolves around them and their environment. As one of them exclaimed in disbelief, "But the whole world didn't even begin until 1492!"[5]

Within a year, all 180 schools in Florida's Broward County school district will be linked in a vast computer network. With 161,000 elementary and secondary students, and 180,000 adult education students, the district is the eighth largest in the nation. "We can see how we could expand curriculum offerings without having to find stand-alone teachers," one for each classroom, said Virgil Morgan, superintendent of schools.[6]

At the Shoreline School District in Seattle, fiberoptic cables—which transmit data as pulses of light at rates as high as 100 million bits a second—will soon enable students and teachers to retrieve articles, video clips, slides, photographs, and sound recordings from a central resource library. Using two-way video, classes and individual teachers will see and interact with others in the same building or across the district.

The National Science Foundation is planning to establish a high-speed national fiber network by the year 2000 to connect all American universities and, perhaps, most secondary schools. Schools using such a network could draw information from virtually any university library in the nation.

Some schools are experimenting with wireless networks that send data over low-power radio waves, while other schools are being designed with networking "plumbing" built in. Wireless networks are more flexible than wired ones, and more expensive.[7]

TELEVISION

Schools may some day have video wallpaper, where images surround students. In the near term the conventional video monitor—or television—will enter most classrooms in updated form. The video monitor will likely be connected to computers, video camcorders, videocassette recorders, laser disks, compact disk players, cable TV, satellite dishes, and even to other classrooms for live, two-way television broadcasts. Eventually, high-definition television using digital signals will bring photographic-quality images to viewers, along with computer data and graphics. Japanese companies have indicated that they plan to integrate computers and optical disks into new monitors, creating video computers. American companies, by contrast, are trying to integrate video into computers, creating multimedia PCs.[8]

MULTIMEDIA AND OPTICAL DISKS

The combination of computer data, graphics, sound, and video is called multimedia and is already being used to convey information. The next step is to give more students the tools to produce their own multimedia presentations.

Optical disks include intriguing technology and will involve computers that can record, erase, and record again on a single optical disk.[9]

SATELLITES AND ELECTRONIC MAIL

The recent development of satellite receiving dishes the size of garbage can lids will eventually allow homes and individual classrooms to pull in signals from satellites. Using portable satellite transmitting stations, professors will be able to beam lectures directly from remote archeological sites to schools, and students on field trips will send in on-site reports.

Electronic mail, or E-mail, enables teachers, administrators, and students to keep in contact more efficiently than if they used postal or inter-office mail, or even the telephone. Electronic messages can be sent at any time and stored in a central computer, to be retrieved at the recipient's convenience.[10]

As usual, the technology is expected to progress much faster than the ability of schools to pay for it. New technologies are always expensive, and schools and legislators will continue to struggle to find innovative and equitable ways to pay for advanced educational tools.[11]

ENDNOTES

1. Lewis, Peter H., "The Technology of Tomorrow," The Principal Magazine, New York, Vol. 71:2, 1991, p. 7.
2. *Ibid.,* p. 71.
3. McCarty, Paul, "Bringing the World Into the Classroom," The Principal Magazine, November, 1991, p. 7.
4. *Ibid.,* p. 7.
5 and 6. Lewis, p. 7.
7 and 8. Lewis, pp. 7 and 8.
9. *Ibid.,* p. 8.
10 and 11. *Ibid.,* p. 8.

QUESTIONS

1. Write two or three paragraphs which explain the advances which modern technology may bring.
2. Explain what World Classroom is and does.

Chapter 28

JOYS IN TEACHING

We have dealt with the rules and restrictions, as well as the legal aspects of teaching, but surely what keeps teachers in the profession year after year is mainly the joys which accompany working with children and young people.

Susan Moore Johnson, who wrote the book, *Teachers at Work*, studied 115 teachers. She found one consistent feature in the fact that there were many of those teachers who were survivors who had persisted in teaching through difficult times, who had returned to teaching after layoffs, and who had watched respected colleagues leave the teaching ranks either by necessity or by choice. Those teachers had a commitment to children and the social purposes of schooling.

She asked that group of teachers if teaching had been the career that they had anticipated. The answer to this very important question was an ambiguous "Yes, but . . . " *Yes,* teachers experience satisfaction in their work with children and believe that their contributions have been meaningful, *but* their teaching careers have also been frustrating and disappointing, and they have not been nearly as effective in their work as they had once hoped.[1]

In recent years both the restrictions which are placed upon teachers in making reports regarding federal funding, and the fact that the schools have been expected to take over many of the functions which formerly were the responsibility of the home, have made for less joy in teaching. Also, it goes without saying that the breakup of homes and of the stability of such formerly stable institutions as the home and church has eroded the basic structure of a formerly highly respected profession and has dulled some of the interest and creativity which had drawn people of quality into teaching. Nevertheless, teachers who have for years felt their work was a "calling" and a challenge continue to testify that the joy of watching students grow and change as they acquire skills and knowledge makes these teachers feel that there are few professions more rewarding.

A teacher who loves teaching will tell you that the joy of experiencing the zest and vitality of young people, of the day-to-day rapport and exchange of ideas, the lively discussions, the interaction with one's peers among the faculty, and working with such a myriad of personalities makes each day full of new experiences. Even the challenges of working on curriculum and textbook committees, and the planning for future educational events can prove to be a joy. Also a "plus" can be working with many of the students' parents where deep friendships can develop.

In Susan Johnson's study of teachers who persisted in teaching, she stated that it was reassuring to hear those teachers speak of the rewards they experience in teaching. Richard Sand, a teacher, said that he was proud to be a teacher, even if society fails to recognize the work, and he is proud that he "can reach a few kids every now and then who, for whatever reason, can't work with somebody else." Another teacher, Allen Rondo, described the rewards of working with a variety of students.

"The job centers around a fascination with kids. And for all the kids I've taught. I can hardly think of two who are really alike.[2]

There is an undeniable rapture in other respondents' remarks to the author as students described what mattered to them, what moved them.

"There's a joy in listening to what children say. The *curiosity* that they have. The way they like to discover. And I like teaching them that way. So I guess that's why I've stayed," replied another respondent.

Others testified:

"There are certain aspects of teaching I love. I love instructing. I love working with kids. I think having been a convert (to teaching) at a later age, my enthusiasm is still there."

"I love the give and take; I love to see the minds grow. I love to see them do what they think they can't do. It's just a challenge."

"I feel a real personal commitment to my kids to give them the best that I can give them. It's very, very important to me."[3]

If one has an Administration which allows one the latitude of being creative, the lasting joys of working with young people can be a rare privilege. Commencement time always pinpoints the satisfactions of having worked for achievement and having attained goals.

Another aspect of enjoyment is the reading in preparation for the actual teaching itself. If one likes to study, it is fascinating to be able to delve into the reading which is connected with a discipline. Broadening one's horizon with travel, and focusing upon the sharing of those travel experiences in the classroom, expands one's horizons and brings en-richening experiences.

Hence, if one's interest is in children and/or young people, there is no end to the fascination and joys which teaching brings as one is on the "growing edge" in keeping alert to what is happening in the daily lives of people and in the wide, wide, wonderful world around us.

QUESTIONS

1. Tell reasons teachers stay in teaching despite frustrations.
2. What are some of the joys and compensations of teaching which you can enumerate.

Chapter 29

LIFELONG LEARNING

One of the greatest assets of the teaching profession is the assignment for the teacher to continually grow and learn. Reading, travel, and new experiences in many areas provide rewards and satisfactions. One is most fortunate if one is in a district that allows credit for professional growth and encourages one to take additional courses in education and to continue to travel as part of one's getting higher on the salary schedule. Lifelong learning, for teachers as well as for others, is a "must."

ADULT EDUCATION

Adult education must be woven into the fabric of our institutional pattern of living. Continuing education must be made as natural as brushing our teeth. And it must be made as readily available as the water we use for brushing them. Learning opportunities for adults must also be made as economical as the toothpaste we purchase. When this is true, adult education will be as fundamental, if not more so, as literacy. Whereas a grade school education was a necessity a generation ago, a high school education is minimal in our society today.[1]

We are by no means an educated people in America, although we have one of the highest ratings in terms of educational opportunities. Data in the United States census report indicates that the percentage of total illiterates dropped from 20 percent in 1870 to 4.3 percent in 1930. "Functional illiteracy" (less than five years of schooling) among adults was lowered from 11 percent in 1950 to 8 percent in 1960. Nearly one fourth of our adult population is poorly educated for this century, according to some estimates. In 1960 it was reported that 8,300,000 adults, 25 years or older, had less than five years of school, and it is estimated that 23,000,000, or 23 percent have had less than eight years of school. Of those with five years of schooling or less, Edward Warner Brice, U.S. Office of Education, estimates that 900,000 of the uneducated adults are 65 years of age or older.[2]

COMMUNITY EDUCATION

Today, schools offer adult education as a community service or in hope of earning sorely needed revenue. In future, they will be teaching adults because they haven't any choice. As a society, we will add that chore to drug and sex education and the hundred other things we now expect of our schools beyond the traditional "three R's."

Community education becomes not just schools opening up their facilities and extending their resources, but an ecosystem of institutions and agencies conscious of their responsibility for developing the knowledge, values, skills, and habits of a free people.

FUTURE TRENDS

The following are considered some of the future trends in education:

1. Education will be the major public agenda item into the twenty-first century.

2. Education will continue to be viewed as the key to economic growth.

3. Technology, coupled with flexible home, work, and learning schedules, will provide more productive time for schooling, training, and working.

4. Three-quarters of new entrants for jobs will be qualified for only 40% of new jobs created between 1985 and 2000.

5. One million youth will continue to drop out of school annually, at an estimated cost of $240 billion in lost earnings and forgone taxes over their lifetimes.

6. The number of at-risk students will increase as academic standards rise and social problems (such as drug abuse, teenage pregnancy) intensify.

7. We will need 2 million new teachers in the public-school system between now and 1995, but historical projections indicate that only a little over a million will materialize.

8. Lifelong learning will generate birth-to-death curriculum and delivery systems.

9. The focus on thinking globally will make foreign languages, particularly French, German, Spanish, Russian and Japanese, a requirement for all students who are entering college programs.

10. Foreign-language and bilingual instruction will become a necessity for all students for the twenty-first century. All states will initiate programs or expand existing ones to prepare students for a world-wide marketplace.

Hence we must make plans for lifelong learning.

Change a child, and he may become a leader; change a Churchill and you change the destiny of the world.[3]

ENDNOTES

1. Axford, Dr. Roger W., *Adult Education* (*The Open Door*), Pennsylvania, International Textbook Co., 1969, pp. 57–58.
2. *Ibid.,* pp. 8–9.
3. *Ibid.,* p. 57.

QUESTIONS

1. Why is lifelong learning essential in the 1990's?
2. How much schooling has a large segment of the adult population in the United States? What provisions are being planned to upgrade the level of education?
3. State at least five future trends which are being predicted regarding the future of education in the U.S.

Chapter 30

THE INDISPENSABLE QUALITIES

A few qualities are indispensable for one to be an effective teacher. Among these are: a sense of humor, flexibility, and concern.

A SENSE OF HUMOR

With this quality, of course, "Either you have it or else you don't." It is an unfortunate person, however, who doesn't. It can make all the difference between enjoying the day-to-day relationships with young people and children and taking them and the day's work so seriously that it is nothing but a bore and a trial. Many pedagogues have found the day's work to be the latter because they lacked this indispensable quality. If one can experience the joy and see the humor in many of the situations in which there is "the human element" his days will be rewarding. I have seen some pedagogues who lacked a sense of humor take themselves and their students so seriously that every small occurrence pained them. This does not mean that one is laughing about every small thing but rather that he maintains a certain distance and perspective whereby he can to himself see an incident in its perspective to time or to the universe and not make major issues out of minor ones.

FLEXIBILITY

Flexibility is a quality which can be developed. Probably the reason many young parents and young pedagogues relate so well to children is that they might possess this quality more than one with more years, although that is not necessarily always true as some older people are flexible and some young people rigid.

It is of vital importance in a school situation to be adjustable to any situation or any occurrence and to change plans and actions to handle or to relate to almost any situation. It has been stressed previously that it is vitally important to have plans and direction, but within that framework it is also vitally important to be able to change them at a moment's notice to direct actions toward the needs of the students.

130

CONCERN

There is another indispensable quality which is a prerequisite for any teacher, and particularly for a teacher who works with the culturally deprived pupil. Without that quality, the teacher will be at a complete loss in attempting to accomplish his task. Without it the teacher will be as "sounding brass and a tinkling cymbal." What is that quality? It is that of *concern,* of understanding, of compassion.

Concern cannot be feigned. The pupil can easily detect whether the teacher's sense of concern is a real one or whether it is just a facade. If it is the latter, the young person will no doubt rebuff or reject the teacher; if, however, it is the former, it is to that kind of teacher, and that kind only, that the student will look for help.

Some teachers, particularly ones new in the field, mistakenly feel that they should identify with teen-agers on their level in order to win their confidence. This is a grave error. It is the person with mature judgment and a sense of integrity whom they admire. Because many young people lack adequate parental guidance, and because many are without wise parental help, some will quickly adopt the teacher within the classroom as a surrogate father or mother. Under the brittle or calloused exterior which they present, many teen-agers are desperately crying out for help, for love, and for proper concern. J. D. Salinger in his best-selling book of a few years ago which has become almost a classic regarding the teen-age world (*Catcher in the Rye*), skillfully depicted Holden Caulfield, whom teen-agers have embraced as typical of their generation and with whom they readily identify because of his desperate and unsuccessful search for someone with understanding, someone with judgment, someone to whom he could talk—just talk!

In *My Shadow Ran Fast,* a book by Bill Sands, he told of the remarkable quality of personal concern exhibited by both Warden and Mrs. Duffy, of San Quentin prison, as they successfully worked in an unbelievably effective way in understanding and rehabilitating "hardened criminals."

In a dramatic fashion, Sands related how, as a young boy, he had lacked proper parental guidance and concern to the point that he became a "thrill bandit" to prove to himself and to others his toughness. After years of unhappiness and of getting into one involvement of trouble after another, which meant heartbreak and led to the death of his father, who had been an eminent judge, and, after becoming involved in a succession of criminal acts, Bill Sands was sentenced to San Quentin prison where he was faced with consecutive prison terms to be served there. He relates in his book how, when he arrived at San Quentin, he became involved in further difficulties which landed him in solitary confinement. All through his young and teen-age years, Bill Sands, who was the product of a divorced home, felt bereft of any person of love and compassion who was interested in him or his problems. Although his father had been concerned with his welfare, he had never successfully established rapport, or communicated in words to him, of his concern. The book is one which tells in detail the problems which led him to the most sordid type of human despair and defeat. He describes how he was filled with revulsion, shame, and self-loathing and wished only for his own death. Then into his life one day when he was confined in solitary, came Warden Clinton T. Duffy. It was through Duffy's expression of concern for him, communicated through his compassionate eyes of blue and his words, "I care," expressed to him, that Sands was inspired to become rehabilitated and arduously to work out for himself a plan of rehabilitation. The stories of Duffy's life of concern for his inmates can be testified to by many others of San Quentin's former inmates; the same quality of concern was possessed by Warden Lewis Lawes who for years helped rehabilitate men at Sing Sing prison in New York state. Countless parole officers and juvenile court judges can testify to the importance of this indispensable quality.

I was a teacher at Palm Springs High and was in a high school assembly where 1600 sophisticated teen-agers were assembled when Bill Sands related to the group the experiences he had had at San Quentin prison and lauded Warden Duffy, as he described the type of sympathetic understanding which Duffy had successfully communicated to him. Probably no group of high school teen-agers is more apparently sophisticated than the ones at Palm Springs High. Yet at the end of the assembly the entire student body cheered and clapped in a five-minute standing ovation in respect and thanks to Bill Sands for the type of presentation he had given. The response from these teen-agers of today revealed to me dramatically the type of personality they truly respect and the qualities which are components of those personalities—a man who had suffered, yet, won over by love and understanding, had become a worker with delinquents and juvenile offenders himself.

A novice teacher, then, may sometimes mistakenly feel that kindness to culturally deprived pupils means an inter-personal relationship which is satisfying to the teacher rather than a real concern as to what will most benefit the pupil presently and in the years to come. The former is a superficial relationship and is a fleeting thing. That type of outlook I would characterize as an immature and unprofessional one. A teacher's personal friendships should be established largely with the faculty group. Real friendships of years standing are satisfyingly established with the students by a teacher's caring more for the youth's welfare than in a fleeting, momentary way. The teacher who has far more gratification is the one who can have students come back to him in after years as real friends to express a deep appreciation for the attitudes and skills which he feels that the teacher has helped him acquire and develop.

The teacher who deeply cares about his pupils, then, will dedicate himself to a task where the satisfactions are not always visible. He will care enough that even if he does not gain the satisfaction of later hearing his students express their gratitude, he will have the inner joy of knowing some of the growth, some of the change of attitudes, and the skills which have been developed, and of knowing that a particular student's future may be always happier and brighter because of him or of his work, and that in the economy of God his efforts are not lost.

QUESTIONS

1. What are some indispensable qualities which are pre-requisites for being a good teacher?
2. How can one best gain the confidence of teen-agers or of children?
3. Do teen-agers seek out one with mature judgment or one who attempts to act in a teen-age manner himself?
4. What kind of friendship or understanding should exist between teacher and pupil?
5. How involved in the personal lives of pupils should a teacher become?
6. What are legal implications which inhibit one from other than a professional relationship, of which every teacher should be cognizant?

BIBLIOGRAPHY

Albert, Linda, *Coping With Kids and School,* New York, E. P. Dutton, 1984.

Allen, Charles M., *Combatting the Drop-Out Problems,* Chicago, Science Research Associates, 1956.

Axford, Roger, *Adult Education (The Open Door),* Scranton, PA, International Textbook, 1969.

Benjamin, Robert, *Making Schools Work,* New York, Continuum, 1981.

Caravello, S. J., "The Drop-Out Problem," *High School Journal,* 41:355–40, May, 1958.

Cetron, Marvin & Gayle, Margaret, *Educational Renaissance,* New York, St. Martin's Press, 1991.

Chubb, John E., & Moe, Terry M., *Politics, Markets, and America's Schools,* Washington, DC, The Brookings Institution, 1990.

Claiborne, Robert, *Saying What You Mean,* New York, W. W. Norton, 1986.

Clark, Joe with Picard, Joe, *Laying Down the Law,* Washington, DC, Regnery Gateway, 1989.

Farber, Barry A., *Crisis in Education,* San Francisco, Jossey-Bass, 1991.

Farris, R. S. "Meeting Their Needs" Columbus, Ohio, Vol. 22:2, Natl. Middle School Assn. November, 1990.

Flexner, Stuart Berg, *I Hear America Talking,* New York, Van Nostrand Reinhold, 1976.

Frady, Marshall & Dunphy, Joan S., *To Save Our Schools, To Save Our Children,* Far Hills, NJ, New Horizon Press, 1985.

Goens, George A., and Clover, Sharon, *Getting the Most From Public Schools,* Florida, Pineapple Press, 1987.

Goodlad, John I., *A Place Called School,* New York, McGraw-Hill, 1984.

Greenberg, Herbert M., *Teaching With Feeling,* New York, Macmillan, 1969.

Halling, Victor J., *Search for Truth: Studies in Psychology,* Dubuque, Iowa, Kendall-Hunt, 1968.

Hayakawa, S. I., *Language in Thought and Action,* New York, Harcourt, Brace, and World, 1964.

Johnson, Susan Moore, *Teachers at Work,* New York, Basic Books, 1990.

Lewis, Peter H., "The Technology of Tomorrow," *The Principal* Magazine, Volume 71:2, November, 1991.

Lockard, Abrams, & Many, *Microcomputers for Educators,* Boston, Little, Brown, 1987.

McCarty, Paul, "Bringing the World Into the Classroom," *The Principal Magazine,* November, 1991.

McClenaghan, Wm. A., *Magruder's American Government,* Boston, Allyn & Bacon, Boston, 1983.

Maeroff, Gene I., *Don't Blame the Kids,* New York, McGraw-Hill, 1982.

Minor, Ed, *Handbook for Preparing Visual Media,* New York, McGraw-Hill, 1978.

Mulligan, William, "A Study of Dyslexia and Delinquency," *Academic Therapy,* Volume IV:3, Spring, 1969.

Newman, Ruth G., *Groups in Schools,* New York, Simon & Schuster, 1974.

Penty, Ruth, *Reading Ability and High School Dropouts,* New York, Teachers' College, Columbia University, 1956.

Schadler, Cliff, *The Principal Magazine,* New York, Yeshiva-Day Schools, Volume 71:4, 1992.

Schimmel, David and Fischer, Louis, *Parents, Schools, and the Law,* (2nd Printing), Columbia, MO, The National Committee for Citizens in Education, 1988.

Schuster, Bob, *Tribune* Newspapers, Arizona, May 3, 1992.

Shepardson, Richard D., *Elementary Teacher's Discipline Desk Book,* West Nyack, NY, Parker Publishing, 1980.

Shepp, D. W., "Can We Salvage the Drop-Outs?" Clearing House, Volume 31: September, 1956.

Strickland, Phillips, and Phillips, *Avoiding Teacher Malpractice,* New York, Hawthorn, 1976.

Tischler, Whitten, and Hunter, *Introduction to Sociology,* New York, Holt, Rinehart, and Winston, 1983.

Ubben, Gerald C., and Hughes, Larry W., *The Principal,* Boston, Allyn & Bacon, 1987.

Walker, Kozma and Green, *American Education,* San Francisco, West, 1989.

INDEX